SPIRIT WORLD

Alan Leonhardt

SPIRIT WORLD

Copyright © 2019 by Alan F. Leonhardt

Published by Lionheart Publications, a division of Lionheart Ministries

1600 W. State Rd
Hastings, MI 49058
alanleonhardt@gmail.com

Printed in the United States of America

All Rights Reserved. No part of this publication may be reproduced, stored in a retrieval system, or transmitted in any form or by any means - for example, electronic, photocopy, and recording - without the prior written permission of the publisher. The only exception is brief quotations in printed reviews.

ISBN 978-0-1234-5678-6
Second Edition June 2019

Unless otherwise indicated, scripture is taken from the New King James Version. Copyright © 1982 Thomas Nelson, Inc. Used by permission. All rights reserved.

Scripture marked NIV is taken from the Holy Bible, New International Version Copyright © 1973, 1978, 1984 by International Bible Society. Used by permission of Zondervan. All rights reserved.

Scripture marked AMP is taken from the Amplified Bible. Copyright © 1954, 1958, 1962, 1964, 1965, 1987 by the Lockman Foundation. Used by permission.

Strong's number references are taken from Strong's Exhaustive Concordance of the Bible, by James Strong.

DEDICATION

I want to dedicate all my books to the next generation.

*One generation shall praise Your works to another,
And shall declare Your mighty acts.* ~Psalm 145:4

We have an obligation to pass on our wisdom and experience to the next generation. My biggest inspirations are my children. I want my ceiling in life to be their starting place and platform. If we are wise, we will admit that we all stand on the shoulders of great men and women who have mentored us with the sacrifice of their lives. If someone can glean some good thing from this book that will help establish them and give them greater endurance to finish their race, then I will have done my job. This being said, there are some very special people I would like to thank:

- I would like to thank my wife Nicole for being brutally honest when I need it, but also a great inspiration and a constant source of encouragement.

- I would like to thank my four daughters, Bethany, Hannah, Ariel and Gabriella. I want to make you proud of your Dad and leave you a good legacy.

- I would like to thank my church family at Hastings Assembly of God. I always tell them to sow grace into the lives of others; you never know when you're going to need some back. Apparently I must have sown some good seed because they continually give grace back to me and my family. They are a great church to pastor.

- I would like to thank my editor, Kathy Mayo. She is such a hard worker and has a servant's heart. She has challenged me to go beyond being a good writer, to becoming a great writer.

- Lastly, I would like to thank Dr. Leon van Rooyen, the President and founder of Global Ministries and Relief. He has been a great friend and mentor. He has this gift of faith and encouragement about him. When I tell him of my big dreams, he doesn't scoff or even flinch. He takes me seriously and does everything within his power to encourage me. He truly invests in my life. Some men achieve greatness by their deeds, others by inspiring others to do great things; Dr. van Rooyen is great because he does both.

REVIEWS

In Pastor Alan's book "Spirit World," he speaks from experience about moving successfully in the Holy Spirit. This is a rare teaching. I highly recommend it.
~ Troy Townsend
Gilead Healing Team
Lansing, MI

First, let me say, I love Spirit World. I just received it and read the first chapter. Wow! Every theological doctrine, including eschatology (the study of end times), in just twenty pages! Amazing and brilliant. I didn't want to stop reading and can't wait now for chapter two and beyond.
~ Dave Williams
Dave Williams Ministries
Lansing, MI

Rev. Leonhardt's book, "Spirit World," is an essential book for your collection on the Holy Spirit. It is well written, insightful, and full of personal stories that make the content come to life. I appreciate that it is Scriptural and practical. It also comes from a life of experience in walking with the Holy Spirit. Pick a copy up for yourself and a friend, today!
~ Chris Palmer
Light of Today Ministries
Farmington Hill, MI

Alan will take you on a fascinating journey through the spirit world as he weaves his own stories with plenty of scripture to back those stories up. Let him take you to what he calls "the God Zone" where you will see what a loving God we serve. You will laugh and you will cry as Alan changes your views on what it truly means to be an "on fire" Christian today.
~ Mark Christensen
Edward Jones Financial Advisor [retired]
Hastings, MI

Contents

Chapter 1
    The Spirit Realm is Real........................... 9

Chapter 2
    The Shattered Box.................................. 31

Chapter 3
    The Still Small Voice................................ 41

Chapter 4
    God's Word is Spirit and Life.................... 63

Chapter 5
    Introduction to Dreams and Visions............ 75

Chapter 6
    The Dream Weaver................................ 83

Chapter 7
    Visions.. 97

Chapter 8
    Spiritual Impartation............................. 113

Chapter 9
    Why do They Speak in Tongues?............... 133

Chapter 10
    Why do I Speak in Tongues?.................... 155

Chapter 11
    Desire to Prophesy............................... 171

Chapter 12
    Spiritual Atmospheres........................... 197

Chapter 13
    Spiritual Warfare................................. 213

Radical Transformation 233

To deny the existence of the spiritual realm is like living in a two-dimensional world.

Chapter 1

THE SPIRIT REALM IS REAL

We lived in a little town called Beulah, Michigan. It was located just south of the Sleeping Bear Sand Dunes National Lakeshore. Winters could be quite challenging with lake effect snow. By mid-winter the accumulated snow on the ground could be three to five feet deep. Make sure your little dog, Fluffy, stays on the shoveled path or you won't find her until spring.

In early spring, the piney woods of northern-lower Michigan are filled with the fresh smell of wild flowers and the melodious sounds of the red-breasted robin. The beauty of the forests, lakes and sand dunes of the western part of the state are a magnet for tourism. Summers are hot and humid. The cool freshwater lakes are major attractions for sportsmen and swimmers. I used to make a campfire on a secluded evening beach of Lake Michigan and let the soothing rhythm of the surf relax me. Living and pastoring a church in this area of Michigan was a dream come true. Even though this was a vacation paradise, evil lurked.

For several mornings my ten-year-old daughter Hannah woke me up with tears in her eyes. She was being tormented in her sleep with nightmares. (Hannah is our number two daughter of four.) Although nightmares are a somewhat common childhood experience, I suspected that this was more than just my child feeling vulnerable and manifesting her fears in the form of nightmares. As a Christian parent, I was discerning a spiritual attack and knew that I wasn't powerless to just let this continue. I began to pray for her before she went to sleep at night. I prayed for a peaceful sleep and commanded fear to go. I quoted the verse in 2 Timothy 1:7, *"For God has not given us a spirit of fear but of power and of love and of a sound mind."* Night after night I prayed with her at her bedside, but the nightmares continued.

One night I was up and awake later than usual. Before I went to bed I thought it would be good to go into Hannah's room and pray over her while she slept. As I came into her room I sensed something evil enter the room; it came right through the outside wall. I didn't see anything, but I felt its presence; my spiritual senses were on high alert. I felt the indignation of the Holy Spirit rise up in me and I was angry. I spoke to that spirit and commanded it by the Holy name of Jesus to leave that room and never come back! Immediately I sensed that the evil presence was gone, and then I worshiped and thanked God. A great peace came into that room. After that confrontation Hannah was free from those nightmares.

My little girl was being attacked and tormented by a nefarious spirit in the night. I didn't believe I had done anything to open my home up to evil spirits, so it was then that I came to believe that demonic forces don't have to have a reason to attack. They will systematically test your defenses to find a way in. If you are ignorant of spiritual warfare or if you don't know your authority in Christ, the demonic hordes from hell will march right over you. The spirit realm is real. 1 Peter 5:8 tells us,

"Be sober, be vigilant; because your adversary the devil walks about like a roaring lion, seeking whom he may devour." There is an invisible kingdom of darkness that unleashes evil and destruction on an unaware mankind. There is also a powerful kingdom of light that can protect us and help us live in victory. God wants to develop our spiritual awareness and discernment so that you and I can navigate successfully through life's greatest challenges. To be in denial of the invisible spiritual realm is to unwittingly be subject to its deadly influences.

THE INVISIBLE CREATED THE VISIBLE

By faith we understand that the worlds were framed by the word of God, so that the things which are seen were not made of things which are visible. ~Hebrews 11:3

As Christians, we must realize that the invisible spirit world exerts tremendous influence on the visible natural world. This isn't some superstitious mumbo jumbo; the spirit world is real. The root cause for many things that we experience, good and bad, are spiritual in nature. To deny the existence of the spiritual realm is like living in a two-dimensional world.

There are many invisible things that we deal with on a daily basis and none of these can be put into a test tube and evaluated by the scientific method. Take, for example, our emotions. Consider what the world would be like if we weren't influenced by the invisible force of our emotions. If emotion suddenly ceased to exist, our lives would be very colorless. Also, invisible emotions can be enriching or toxic; so, too, can the spiritual realm be a source of life, or a deceptive place that yields death. The spiritual realm is also something we interact with every day. Reality is not limited to your five senses. The Bible teaches us how to successfully navigate our spiritual lives. The Bible also teaches that God

SPIRIT WORLD

and the spiritual realm existed before the material universe. The spirit world is eternal, and the material universe is temporary and subject to change. The things which are seen were not made of things which are visible. If all that exists came from God Almighty, who is a spiritual being, then we need to take spiritual things seriously. The invisible spirit world influences your life.

> *While we do not look at the things which are seen, but at the things which are not seen. For the things which are seen are temporary, but the things which are not seen are eternal.*
> *~2 Corinthians 4:18*

The invisible created all things that are visible. God, who is a spiritual being, created everything from nothing. For our reality to exist there must be a "time, space, and mass continuum". There must be space for mass to exist in and there must be a time for it all to occur. This continuum had to come into existence simultaneously. Genesis 1:1 tells us of the creation of the time/space/mass continuum. *"In the beginning (time) God created the heavens (space) and the earth (mass)."* The universe is a trinity of trinities. Time is past, present and future. Space is height, width and depth. Mass is solid, liquid and gas. The God of the Bible transcends time, space and mass. By "transcends" we mean that the God of the Holy Bible is not subject to the laws of this universe. He is eternal and therefore transcends time; time is subject to Him. He is omnipresent so He transcends space. He is above and beyond, and yet the sustainer and glue that holds the universe together. Only an eternal, omnipresent, omnipotent being could have created all that exists. Only the Judeo/Christian God of the Bible fits the description of the logical source of the universe. From the invisible came all that is visible. The spirit world is the source of the entire created order.

> *For, since the creation of the world, His invisible attributes are clearly seen, being understood by the things that are made, even His eternal power and Godhead, so that they are without excuse.* ~Romans 1:20

> *Who being the brightness of His glory and the express image of His person, and upholding all things by the word of His power, when He had by Himself purged our sins, sat down at the right hand of the Majesty on high.* ~Hebrews 1:3

Not only has God, who is a spiritual being (see John 4:24), created all that is out of nothing, but He also is active in sustaining the universe through Jesus Christ. I was in a physics class in college and we were studying the atom and atomic science. As the professor droned on about the protons and neutrons orbiting around the atom a thought occurred to me. So I raised my hand and asked why the protons and electrons didn't fly off. What kept them in orbit around the atom? His answer made me laugh. He said that no one truly understands why the atom holds together, it's called Atomic Glue. I immediately thought of a verse in the book of Colossians that speaks of Christ:

> *And He Himself existed before all things, and in Him all things consist (cohere, are held together).* ~Colossians 1:17 AMP

If God, who is spirit, created and sustains all the created order, then the spirit world is even more real than the material world. The spiritual realm holds great sway over our life and world. It's time we accept the truthful claims of the Bible about spiritual realities.

Some folks have such a hard time with supernatural and spiritual things. There is always an attempt to rationalize, or explain away, any miracle or healing. The Gospel of John records an incident when God spoke in an audible voice to a crowd of people and some rationalized that the sound was thunder (see John 12:29). Let's face it, supernatural things scare people. It's just our nature to be afraid of things we don't understand or can't control. Another reason we want to rationalize miracles from God is because to acknowledge them means we acknowledge the existence of the God of the Bible. To do so would be to admit that we are accountable to Him. This is a very tenuous situation for someone who is rebelling against God.

Jesus warned us to beware of the leaven of the Sadducees (see Matthew 16:6). Jesus compared the doctrine of the Sadducees to leaven (see Matthew 16:12) or yeast that you work into dough until all of the bread is infected. What was the doctrine of the Sadducees? The Sadducees did not believe in angels or the resurrection (see Acts 23:8). In fact, they did not believe in the supernatural at all. The Sadducee leaven is still trying to infiltrate the church today. This corrupt reasoning goes along these lines: Because it's impossible for these miraculous stories in the Bible to be true, then the Bible is a book of Jewish mythology that has a moral lesson or truth. The Bible makes no sense when you start surgically removing all supernatural demonstrations. If you take out the supernatural from the Word of God then you are left with a concordance and some maps wrapped in a leather cover.

The leaven of the Sadducees can be more insidious than overtly denying anything spiritual. Churches can begin to suppress any demonstration of the Spirit of God. We can say that we are spiritual and believe all the miracles written in the Bible but deny that God works miracles today! We have just become practical Sadducees, suppressing anything that might stun or convict an unlearned visitor. We are then tempted to think that people are more impressed with an intellectual argument than a demonstration of the power of God.

And my speech and my preaching were not with persuasive words of human wisdom, but in demonstration of the Spirit and of power, that your faith should not be in the wisdom of men but in the power of God. ~1 Corinthians 2:4-5

My Grandmother was a wonderful Christian woman, but she prided herself in being an intellectual and was susceptible to the leaven of the Sadducees. I often visited her in an assisted living home, and although she was over ninety years old at the time she was still sharp as a tack. She was very happy and proud that I was studying to be a minister. She would read these crazy things and wait for me to visit so she could astound and stump me. Once she showed me an article that declared "they" knew where the Children of Israel had crossed the Red Sea. The reason this had to be the spot was because the water there is only SIX INCHES DEEP. I yelled out. "Praise the Lord Grandma!" She asked, "Why are you responding that way? I thought you would be upset that they gave a rational answer that explains one of the greatest miracles of the Bible?" To which I responded, "No Grandma, I think it's awesome how God miraculously drowned a whole Egyptian army in just six inches of water! Think of it! It's a miracle!"

I tried to explain to her that when you try to explain away the miraculous of the Bible, you will end up looking foolish. You only have two choices: either you believe in the miraculous, or you don't. If you choose not to believe in the miraculous then the Bible makes no sense. I would say that you can't even be a Christian without accepting the miraculous. Without believing in miracles how could the Son of God be born of a virgin, live a sinless life, die vicariously for the sins of the world, rise from the dead, be seated at the right hand of God and come again to rule and judge the world? AND…Jesus is still working signs, wonders and miracles through His church today!

Have we lost touch with our connection to the spirit world? Indigenous tribal peoples and third world peoples are very aware of the interrelations we have with powerful spiritual forces. Although some are ignorant of the true nature of those spiritual forces, they at least are keen about the influence they exert. In today's Christian world, third world believers have no problem with the spiritual side of Christianity. They have seen the reality of demon possession, witch doctors and curses. They understand and are so appreciative of the protection and deliverance offered in Christ. Many are so grateful to be rescued from real evil spiritual oppression and to be safe under the shadow of God's wings.

In the western world, Christians who claim that some sicknesses are directly caused by demonic oppression, or that God spoke to them in a dream or by a still small voice, are sometimes viewed as fringe, or somewhat kooky. But what does the Bible say? Are these experiences validated by the Word of God? The Bible is our final authority to validate spiritual experience, not the traditions of men. According to the Bible, the devil and demons are real! Jesus talked about the devil more than anyone in the entire Bible. Jesus was a frontline combatant with malignant spiritual forces. He went about preaching and teaching the gospel of the kingdom, healing every sickness and every disease, and casting out demons (see Matthew 4:23-24).

Do I have to commit intellectual suicide to be a spiritual person? No. It IS possible to be thinking, reasoning Christian, who is solid in character and doctrine, and also be spiritually aware and spiritually discerning. The last thing I want to be is someone who has a powerful argument but no spiritual power to back it up, having an outward form of godliness but denying the power of the Holy Spirit (see 2 Timothy 3:5). I am glad that the power of God helps me to be a better person, but just being a good person isn't good enough. I also need the power of the Holy Spirit to combat evil, spiritual forces, and to help get others set free!

MAN IS A SPIRITUAL BEING

Now may the God of peace Himself sanctify you completely; and may your whole spirit, soul, and body be preserved blameless at the coming of our Lord Jesus Christ.
~1 Thessalonians 5:23

The human make-up is a trichotomy. We are a spirit being, that has a soul, that lives in a body. Our spirit is the place of conscience, intuition and worship. Our soul is the seat of our personality, our mind, will and emotional make-up. Our bodies connect us to this world with our five senses; sight, hearing, taste, touch and smell. Of all the animals on planet earth, mankind is the only being with a spiritual capacity. This sets us apart from the rest of creation. We have a nature to worship, we have a conscience, and we can connect to the spirit world. We were created to have a relationship with God, who is a Spirit (see John 4:24). We were created to connect with both the spirit realm and the natural realm.

Have you ever had a moment of spiritual clarity and awareness? Even before I became a born-again Christian I had lucid spiritual moments when I could sense the presence of God. I can recall one experience when I was young sitting on my friend's front porch. I was waiting for him to come outside and, looking up, I noticed how beautiful the full moon was in the bright blue summer sky. I was enamored with the power and immensity of creation. I sensed God at that moment. I knew He existed and was reaching out to me. I never forgot that feeling of total peace and awareness. God was not only all powerful but He was all good and wanted relationship with little ol' me.

Have you ever sensed the presence of total evil? I'm talking about malignant spiritual forces present and ready to do harm. I was a teenager and taking a girl home from a date late at night and, as we passed by a

SPIRIT WORLD

cemetery on a lonely country road, three men stood in the road and tried to wave us down to stop the car. Immediately I sensed something so evil and terrifying that it almost paralyzed me. The girl I was with began to scream and yell out, "DON'T STOP! DON'T STOP!" I slammed down my foot on the gas pedal and the car roared on through those men; two of them jumped out of the way or they would have become road pizza. Later that week we heard reports of animal sacrifices and graves being dug up and looted in that cemetery.

When the Bible refers to the eternal inner man, it many times lumps the spirit and soul together.

- The spirit is referred to the whole inner man - James 2:26
- The soul is referred to the whole inner man - Mark 8:36
- The heart is designated as the whole inner man - Matthew 22:37

The inner, non-corporeal, heart of man is a soul and a spirit. This soul/spirit is eternal and will live on after the death of your body. For the Christian, the inner man will go directly to heaven to be with Jesus. *"…to be absent from the body is to be present with the Lord" (2 Corinthians 5:8)*. While we are enjoying heaven we will await the resurrection of our bodies. The trumpet will sound and those who have died in Christ will rise first; those Christians who are alive at that time will be immediately transformed into resurrected bodies and will rise to meet Jesus in the air (see 1 Thessalonians 4:13-18 and 1 Corinthians 15:50-58). This event is commonly called the Rapture and is part of the Second Coming of Christ. The Second Coming of Christ happens in two phases: First Jesus comes for His Church (an event known as the Rapture), and then He comes with His church to rule and reign (see Revelation 19).

I remember how freaked out I was when I was first introduced to what the Bible taught about the Rapture. I was 22 years old and playing music in a Christian coffee house. There was a huge mural on one of the walls of the coffee house of Jesus coming back on the clouds. He was in a white robe with a golden sash, and the armies of heaven followed riding white horses. As I was admiring the artwork, the man who ran the coffee house explained that the mural was an artist's portrayal of Jesus coming back WITH His church. He then went on to explain the teaching of the Rapture when Jesus comes back FOR the church. I was completely flabbergasted. I remember saying to him, "Wait a minute, that is in the Bible? Do we really believe that? Are you telling me that we're all going to fly up in the air like Peter Pan?" He then proceeded to show me the Bible verses that explain the Rapture of the church.

That night I was lying in a bunk bed at the coffee house contemplating the rapture and the second coming of Christ. I was trying to imagine how the trumpet of God would sound and then the sudden sensation of being sucked up into the heavens. As I was crossing over into dreamland a midnight train came chugging down the tracks just behind the coffee house. Just as the 5,000-ton caravan barrel rolled on by, the mega horns blew long and loud. I jumped up out of my bunk bed and yelled, "THE RAPTURE!" The guy in the bunk below me yelled back, "SHUT UP, IT'S JUST A TRAIN!" We had a good laugh and went back to sleep. I'm still laughing about it to this day.

> *Beloved, now we are children of God; and it has not yet been revealed what we shall be, but we know that when He is revealed, we shall be like Him, for we shall see Him as He is. And everyone who has this hope in Him purifies himself, just as He is pure.* ~1 John 3:2-3

The Bible says that we will be raised in a glorious spiritual body and raised in power (see 1 Corinthians 15:42-46). We have no idea what kind of powerful spiritual beings we will become. 1 John 3:2 says that we will be like Jesus. What was Jesus like when He rose from the dead? He ate fish and honeycomb. He appeared and disappeared at will, He passed through a wall, and yet He could be touched. Somehow the natural laws did not apply to an immortal spiritual body. On His last day on earth after His resurrection He floated up into the clouds and was seated at the right hand of God. Man, am I going to have fun in my resurrected, eternal body (see Acts 1:9-11 and Luke 24:36-43). Wooo Hooo!

> *But we all, with unveiled face, beholding as in a mirror the glory of the Lord, are being transformed into the same image from glory to glory, just as by the Spirit of the Lord.*
> *~2 Corinthians 3:18*

> *Therefore, we do not lose heart. Even though our outward man is perishing, yet the inward man is being renewed day by day.*
> *~2 Corinthians 4:16*

The inner, eternal man is being transformed into something glorious. If we could be allowed to get even a short glimpse of the luminous spiritual beings that we will emerge into, we would be dumbfounded. We will be transformed from one species to another. Like a caterpillar in metamorphosis, we will one day ascend into a beautiful heavenly being. We cannot completely grasp what we will become, but we know that we shall be like Him, for we shall see Him as He is.

THE WORD OF GOD DISCERNS WHAT IS OF THE SPIRIT AND WHAT IS OF THE SOUL

> *For the word of God is living and powerful, and sharper than any two-edged sword, piercing even to the division of soul and spirit, and of joints and marrow, and is a discerner of the thoughts and intents of the heart.* ~Hebrews 4:12

The Word of God has the ability to help us discern what is of the spirit, and what is of the soul. When talking about the soul here, the Bible is speaking of fleshly carnal desires as opposed to spiritual desires. Baby Christians and carnal Christians have difficulty discerning whether their feelings are of the flesh or spirit. Let me illustrate with this story: *I was a very young believer in Christ and I came to church late. The worship was in full swing and when I entered the sanctuary I felt uncomfortable and wanted to leave. It was strange to me that I had repulsive feelings about being in the worship service, so instead of leaving I stayed and analyzed what was going on. The longer I stayed the more I grew accustomed to the worship and the presence of God. I then realized that those negative feelings I was having when I entered the sanctuary were my flesh (sinful nature). My flesh was resisting the powerful presence of God. As I disciplined my flesh to come under the new spiritual nature in Christ I became more comfortable in the service.*

The whole experience made me wonder, how many times had I obeyed a NEGATIVE feeling and missed God? How many times had I sensed something POSITIVE from the Spirit of God, ignored it and missed God? We need to have discernment to tell whether something is of the flesh or the spirit.

When the angel visited Mary, the mother of Jesus, she was afraid. One of the first things the angel Gabriel told her was to not be afraid. Many assume that because they become afraid of a supernatural experience with God, their fear is the indicator as to whether that experience is valid. Angel visitations are not normal for most of us. I would venture to say that most of us would be a little freaked out, maybe even afraid and shaking in our proverbial boots. God has to help us discern our feelings. Are we just apprehensive about a supernatural manifestation or are we sensing something that is not God?

SPIRIT WORLD

Many times unlearned people visit a church that allows the supernatural experiences of tongues and prophecy. These churches are generally called Pentecostal or Charismatic. If the person visiting for the first time feels uncomfortable in the meeting they may conclude that these gifts of the Holy Spirit are not for today, or not from God. People base their theology on how THEY feel and what is comfortable to THEM, and not on the Word of God which has the authority and power to discern what is of the soul or what is of the spirit.

I often hear folks spiritualize fleshly feelings. If they feel jealous or envious they will conclude that there is something wrong with that person and God is giving them discernment. They will tell you they can't necessarily put their finger on what is wrong with said person but "watch 'em." On the flip side they may be getting a warning from the Spirit of God. We definitely need to develop discernment to tell the difference between what is of the soul (feelings and vain imaginations) and what is true discernment coming from the new spiritual nature in Christ.

How can we develop greater spiritual discernment? It's only through the Word of God, which is sharper than any two-edged sword, that we are able to make distinctions.

> *For everyone who partakes only of milk is unskilled in the word of righteousness, for he is a babe. But solid food belongs to those who are of full age, that is, those who by reason of use have their senses exercised to discern both good and evil.*
> *~Hebrews 5:13-14*

Those who come to a full age of maturity in Christ are those who are skilled in the Word of righteousness. They have worked the word, and through experience have their discernment fine-tuned. Will Rogers (1879-1935), the political humorist once said, "Good judgment comes from experience, and a lot of that comes from bad judgment." There are no shortcuts to having a good grasp on the Bible. You must strive to read it daily. Only the Bible has absolute moral truth. Only the Bible can teach us right from wrong. There will come a day when God's great and precious promises will mean more to you than your necessary food. When you are going through a great testing and trial you learn that hope comes from the God of hope. You discover that truly man does not live by bread alone, but by every word that proceeds from the mouth of God. But if you don't know about those great and precious promises how will you draw strength from them in a time of need? Study the Bible like your life depends on it, because it does.

When I think about the sword of the Spirit, which is the word of God (see Ephesians 6:17), I am reminded of an Old Testament story about David's mighty men. Among the elite warriors of David's kingdom there were several legendary figures that performed great exploits. The number two elite warrior in the realm was a man named Eleazar (see 2 Samuel 23:9-10). The Bible tells us that when there was a battle with the Philistines that the men of Israel retreated. Eleazar arose and attacked! He fought so long and hard, cutting, slashing and thrusting with his sword that he was froze in battle mode. They had to pry his hands from the sword. *"The Lord brought about a great victory that day; and the people returned after him only to plunder."* This is why Eleazar was a mighty man; he arose and attacked when others retreated. Everyone reaped the spoils of his great single-handed victory. Well, it wasn't completely single-handed because God was with him.

Have you ever been alone in a spiritual fight? This is what separates the men from the boys, the women from the girls. Mighty warriors arise and attack when others retreat. If no one is with you and all abandon you, you are still not alone. The God of the angel armies has promised that He will never leave you nor forsake you. Take the sword of the Spirit and stand your ground. Parry and thrust, cut, slash and bludgeon with your sword. Quote the word! Declare the Word! Prophesy the Word! Some battles are long and hard fought, but God will bring about a great victory and many will reap the spoils. People will be encouraged to pick up their swords and fight!

The Word of God is a powerful spiritual weapon. Not only will it build discernment between good and evil, right and wrong, clean and unclean, but it is a game changer. There is no way you can defeat a supernatural spiritual enemy with physical weapons. The veteran spiritual Christian is feared in hell and known in heaven. He knows Jesus and he knows how to use his sword. He practices daily. Every soldier knows that you take care of your weapon. Your weapon is your life.

SPIRITUAL AUTHORITY

Then the seventy returned with joy, saying, "Lord, even the demons are subject to us in Your name." And He said to them, "I saw Satan fall like lightning from heaven. Behold, I give you the authority to trample on serpents and scorpions, and over all the power of the enemy, and nothing shall by any means hurt you. Nevertheless, do not rejoice in this, that the spirits are subject to you, but rather rejoice because your names are written in heaven." ~Luke 10:17-20

As devoted followers of Christ we have authority in the spirit realm. Jesus had His own school of supernatural training. He would delegate spiritual authority to His disciples and then send them out in pairs to expand His ministry to the masses. Jesus could only be in one place at one time and the need was too immense for even Him. This is one of the reasons Jesus told His disciples that it was advantageous for Him to leave them and go to Heaven because then the Holy Spirit could come and enable all the disciples to do the works of Christ (see John 16:7).

Instead of Jesus being the only anointed one there would be hundreds, thousands and millions. The Greek word for Christ means anointed one. If you are a Christian, you are not only a follower of Christ you are a little anointed one; anointed to be an imitator of Jesus and destroy all the works of the devil (see 1 John 3:8). You have delegated spiritual authority and you have been given power over a mighty spiritual enemy.

The disciples had authority over demons in Jesus' name. The name of Jesus is the Power of Attorney in the spiritual realm. When you pray or command in His name, you are saying, "By the authority of the person who bears this name." We have delegated authority in the spirit through the authority of the name of Jesus. When I baptize in the name of Jesus, I am baptizing by the authority of Jesus. If I end my prayer with the phrase "In the name of Jesus", I am praying with the authority of Jesus and I have legal rights to access heaven's throne through Christ's shed blood.

To have the right to use the name of Jesus we must be under the authority of Jesus. If we try to operate outside of the boundaries of the Word of God, or try to assert our own will on a situation, we will fail. The power and authority of heaven will not work for us if we try to operate outside of God's will. We must be under authority to have authority. The book of Acts tells a story of seven sons of a priest who tried to use the name of Jesus to cast a demon out of someone and the demon possessed person rose up and gave them a good thrashing until they were bloodied, bruised and naked (see Acts 19:13). True authority in the spirit realm is reserved for humble followers of Christ. For those whose names are written in the Lamb's Book of Life. It's not for someone who just wants to be on some witchcraft power surge, asserting their own will instead of carrying out the mission of Christ to see people set free from demonic oppression. *"Therefore submit to God. Resist the devil and he will flee from you" (James 4:7).* If we are under God's authority then the devil must flee in terror from us.

Jesus said in Luke 10:19, *"Behold, I give you the authority to trample on serpents and scorpions, and over all the power of the enemy, and nothing shall by any means hurt you."* Serpents and scorpions are emblems of evil spirits in the Bible and we have authority to trample on them; they are under our feet. Romans 16:20 tells us, *"And the God of peace will crush Satan under your feet shortly."* As Joshua was conquering the Promised Land, five kings unified to defeat the children of Israel. God did a miracle and caused the sun to stand still at the prayer of Joshua, and it stood still for about a whole day (see Joshua 10:12-14). The five Amorite kings hid in a cave When Joshua found them he had them brought out to lie face down before the captains of the army. Then Joshua had the captains put their feet on the necks of those kings before he had them executed.

> *"Come near, put your feet on the necks of these kings." And they drew near and put their feet on their necks. Then Joshua said to them, "Do not be afraid, nor be dismayed; be strong and of good courage, for thus the LORD will do to all your enemies against whom you fight."* ~Joshua 10:24-25

This was a powerful, psychological demonstration. Don't be intimidated by spiritual enemies and demonic attacks. Jesus has triumphed over the devil and his forces. Jesus said we have authority over ALL the power of the enemy and NOTHING shall by any means harm us.

> *It is the glory of God to conceal a matter, but the glory of kings is to search out a matter.* ~Proverbs 25:2

I've always had many questions and I am not afraid to talk to God about things that bother me. It's the glory of kings to search out a matter that God has concealed. After I ask God a question, I wait for an answer. I will never cease to be amazed at how God chooses to reveal an answer.

We must realize that there are some questions that cannot be answered this side of heaven. Deuteronomy 29:29 says *"The secret things belong to the LORD our God, but those things which are revealed belong to us and to our children forever, that we may do all the words of this law."* The Almighty is a great revealer of secrets and the things He chooses to reveal will belong to you and your children forever. When you get a revelation from God it becomes part of you and it belongs to you. No one can take that revelation from you.

I don't always tell others my questions lest they mock me. There was one such question that I had concerning our authority in the spirit realm, "Why do demons have to obey me when I use my authority in Christ? I mean, what happens in the spirit world when I pray and command with authority?" In an armed robbery the gun would back up the authority of the robber. If you didn't give the robber what he wanted he could do great physical harm with that weapon. "So, what exactly backs up the authority of Christians, and what does it look like?" (I warned you that I am a little weird. My questions are probably not normal; this is why I don't usually tell folks my questions.)

After I ask a question, I wait on God for the answer. Sometimes I even forget that I asked. I was a member of a Christian rock band that was asked to perform at an outdoor Jesus festival. Folks camped out for days to hear the good music and preaching. I was visiting some of my camping friends and, as we sat around the campfire, a prayer burden came upon us. We gathered in a circle and prayed for the festival and for souls to be saved. You could just sense the presence and power of God on us and around us. As we continued praying I had a vision. It was like the spirit realm was opened up in front of me and I could see what was happening. As the invisible world around me became visible I saw multi-colored lightning flashes rippling across the sky. I could hear

SPIRIT WORLD

the loud thunder claps in full intense surround-sound. Then the Holy Spirit impressed upon me that this is what happens in the spirit realm when God's people pray. God backs up the authority of Christians with real power. Then I heard the Lord say in my spirit, "If you were a demon would you want to stay in that?"

Later that evening, I challenged the Lord about the vision I had received. I asked the Lord to back up what I saw with scripture verses in the Bible. I believe every vision should be subject to the authority of scripture. I was led to the fourth chapter of the book of Revelation:

> *And from the throne preceded lightnings, thunderings, and voices. Seven lamps of fire were burning before the throne, which are the seven Spirits of God.* ~Revelation 4:5

There seems to be times when the power of God manifests as lightnings and thunderings in the spirit world. Since that experience I've found several other scriptures that have backed up my vision and experience:

> *Now all the people witnessed the thunderings, the lightning flashes, the sound of the trumpet, and the mountain smoking; and when the people saw it, they trembled and stood afar off.*
> *~Exodus 20:18*

> *The LORD thundered from heaven,*
> *And the Most High uttered His voice.*
> *He sent out arrows and scattered them;*
> *Lightning bolts, and He vanquished them.* ~2 Samuel 22:14-15

> *Flash forth lightning and scatter them;*
> *Shoot out Your arrows and destroy them.* ~Psalm 144:6

As Christians we should never doubt that God loves us and has given us delegated authority over evil spiritual forces. He has promised in Luke 10:19 that *"Nothing shall by any means harm you."*

As we continue in our journey and discovery of the spirit world, it is very important that we have foundational truths in place. First of all, every experience must be backed up by scripture and can never offend the revealed character of God. Secondly, when we are right with God and under His authority we have nothing to fear because all the force and power of heaven stands behind you. We are under Jesus and His mission, and Jesus is over all. Along with the great commission, Jesus gave us authority and spiritual power to carry it out.

> *By faith we understand that the worlds were framed by the word of God, so that the things which are seen were not made of things which are visible.* ~Hebrews 11:3

Everything that God communicates to us will never contradict the Bible.

Chapter 2

THE SHATTERED BOX

My wife asked me to take her to a conference. Every once in a while, we need to go someplace and get spiritually refreshed. Most people like little weekend getaway vacations, but we mostly prefer a Christian conference with powerful speakers, great worship and prayer times. We don't consider ourselves more spiritual then others by going to faith filled events, just needier.

I asked my wife about the conference and she informed me that it was a prophetic conference. In my mind I was thinking that this would have a lot of teachings about end-time prophecy. All righty then, this should be a little more cerebral than usual. Maybe I'll have some of my Bible prophecy questions answered. When we arrived at the conference I realized this was not what I was expecting. This was about the prophetic movement and modern-day prophets, not end-time prophecy.

The prophetic crowd in Pentecostal/Charismatic circles is a little different. I would classify them as the free-spirited neo-hippies of the contemporary church. Many brought djembe drums and rain sticks.

SPIRIT WORLD

When you shake someone's hand they may hold on a little longer than what's comfortable and look at you with glazed over eyes. You get a sense that they're trying to peer into your soul and get a read on you. It can be a bit creepy and disconcerting. I've grown accustomed to this crowd; it's like walking the streets of New York City, the strangely dressed and bizarre become part of the blended landscape, mostly harmless, so you just walk on by.

The flag wavers were there as well. During worship they danced and spun their colorful banners like a drum majorette or a ninja fighter. I got too close to one once and made the mistake of closing my eyes during worship. I heard a faint whistle and felt a slight breeze as the flag on a stick missed my face by millimeters. It didn't take my lightning fast brain long to realize I should probably keep my eyes open while worshiping. It would be awkward coming home from a conference and having a parishioner ask, "Did you receive anything from the conference?" To which my response would be, "Yeah, I received a bruised forehead while worshiping. A ninja banner waver whacked me good." I don't have anything against banner waving in services as long as the section is large enough for their artistic gyrations.

During this conference, private prophetic sessions for full-time Christian workers were offered. All you had to do was sign up and they would put you in a slot. I was told that we would have a private meeting with a group of four or five prophets/prophetesses and they would encourage us with prophetic words and visions. This sounded a little sketchy but hey, I'll try anything once. My wife Nicole and I went to our appointment and sat down at a table with five other people who were designated to prophecy to us. There weren't any pleasantries as they got right down to business. The leader grabbed a hand-held recording device and stated his name, date, the name of the conference and our names. Then they all sat quietly and stared at us. As they passed the recording device around, each took a turn and described a visual picture or prophetic insight they were getting about us and our ministry. I have to say, they were right on. The insights they received were amazing.

The leader of the group looked at me and told me that he saw a beautiful ornate box in his mind's eye. The hand of God came down and shattered the box into a thousand shards. He told me that I had God in a box and that God was going to shatter my limited view of how God speaks to us. New prophetic insights and experiences were coming my way. I told him that I was open but measured everything by the Word of God. He gave me a half smile and sort of chuckled like he knew something I didn't.

THE VISION OF THE HUMMINGBIRD

As we sat in front of this prophetic group of both men and women, the leader ended with one last odd prophetic word that I still ponder. He said, "As I consider your ministry the image of an eagle appeared and then a circle with an angled line through it. Although the eagle is a noble symbol of our faith, and we are to soar high like an eagle on the wind, it's NOT the eagle. Then I saw a honey bee followed by a circle with a line through it. Although we are to be busy as a bee, the symbol for your ministry is NOT a bee. Then I saw a hummingbird. The hummingbird is an amazing bird. It is considered an engineering impossibility for it to fly, and yet the hummingbird migrates thousands of miles each year. It has the ability to hover and to go into reverse. It has a greater range of motion than any other bird. It can change directions quickly to get to the nectar. The Holy Spirit wants to speak to you about the hummingbird and how that relates to your ministry."

SPIRIT WORLD

As time went on I continued to muse about the man's vision of the hummingbird. This would be one of my first lessons on some of the ways that God speaks. I never would have thought that God wanted to reveal things to me by considering a bird. It makes sense though; Jesus used agriculture parables illustrating life lessons through seedtime, harvest and nature. Throughout the Bible God used nature as metaphors, similes and illustrations.

Here are a few Bible verses that tell us that God can speak through nature:

> *But now ask the beasts, and they will teach you; and the birds of the air, and they will tell you;*
> *Or speak to the earth, and it will teach you; and the fish of the sea will explain to you.* ~Job 12:7-8

> *The heavens declare the glory of God; and the firmament shows His handiwork.*
> *Day unto day utters speech, and night unto night reveals knowledge.* ~Psalm 19:1-2

> *For since the creation of the world His invisible attributes are clearly seen, being understood by the things that are made, even His eternal power and Godhead, so that they are without excuse.* ~Romans 1:20

One hot summer evening I held a board meeting with the deacons of the church I was pastoring. This was just a couple of months after Nicole and I had been to the prophetic conference. We had to open the windows and doors of the classroom we were meeting in because there was no central air-conditioning in this particular church. As we began the meeting a hummingbird flew into the midst of us and hovered over the center of the table for a few seconds. As the bird hovered around the room one of the deacons caught it in an empty plastic ice cream bucket and let it go outside, unharmed. I was dumbfounded. I knew this wasn't just a chance occurrence. God was confirming the prophet's hummingbird vision. God still had some things to say to me through this symbol and I was to continue to seek understanding.

A few weeks after that incident I was talking to a friend in the church parking lot after a Sunday morning service. This friend was a very prophetic person and was well versed in the ways of the strange and bizarre. (He was one of those neo-hippy prophets I mentioned earlier.) My wife Nicole was with us and we were standing in a circle discussing the vision of the hummingbird. I was also relating what happened at the deacon meeting where the hummingbird flew right into the midst of the meeting and hovered over the table. Just then we heard the sound of loud humming and a beautifully colored hummingbird flew and hovered right in the center of the three of us. As we glared with our mouths gaping, the bird shot straight upward with incredible speed and out of sight.

I think that some things are meant for us to ponder, to think on and glean new insight for years to come. There are two incidents in the Bible where God revealed something that needed long-term reflection. While some folks quickly dismiss things, others have a spiritual sensitivity that says, "You may not understand this right now but pay attention." The first reference is in the book of Genesis where Joseph told his father and brothers some of his dreams.

> *Then he dreamed still another dream and told it to his brothers, and said, "Look, I have dreamed another dream. And this time, the sun, the moon, and the eleven stars bowed down to me." So he told it to his father and his brothers; and his father rebuked him and said to him, "What is this dream that you have dreamed? Shall your mother and I and your brothers indeed come to bow down to the earth before you?"*

SPIRIT WORLD

> *And his brothers envied him, but his father kept the matter in mind.*
> *~Genesis 37:9-11*

Notice how Joseph's father Jacob kept the matter in his mind while the brothers couldn't see past their envy. Jacob was spiritually sensitive and sensed that God was speaking prophetically through Joseph's dreams. He may not have understood the meaning, but he knew that God would reveal secrets in His own time. Therefore, Jacob kept the matter in the back of his mind.

The second time something of a similar nature happened was with Mary, the mother of Jesus, when the shepherds came to worship Jesus in the manger. The shepherds revealed to Mary and Joseph what the angels had told them concerning Jesus. Mary stored away in her heart all the strange prophetic occurrences that transpired when Jesus was born. I'm almost certain Mary could not grasp the scope and full significance of what God was trying to say. The life of Jesus would be God's ultimate revelation and expression of Himself (see Hebrews 1:1-3). Some expressions of God deserve long term pondering.

> *And they came with haste and found Mary and Joseph, and the Babe lying in a manger. Now when they had seen Him, they made widely known the saying which was told them concerning this Child. And all those who heard it marveled at those things which were told them by the shepherds. But Mary kept all these things and pondered them in her heart. Then the shepherds returned, glorifying and praising God for all the things that they had heard and seen, as it was told them.*
> *~Luke 2:15-20*

As I further thought and prayed about the vision of the hummingbird I discovered some new insight. First of all, the hummingbird is a symbol of hope, endurance, joy and new beginnings. This is a characteristic of my ministry. When I teach and preach the Word of God, great hope, joy and strength is released. Before I even knew I was called to be a Bible teacher I received a prophecy from a reputable prophet, Dick Mills. He picked me out of a meeting and had me stand up, and then gave me three scriptures with a prophetic word. This was the characteristic of his ministry; he always gave Bible verses with prophetic words. Dick Mills' memory and knowledge of Bible verses and their corresponding addresses was nothing short of astounding. He was like a walking Bible concordance. Here are the three verses Dick Mills gave me that day:

> *The Lord GOD has given me the tongue of the learned, that I should know how to speak a word in season to him who is weary. He awakens me morning by morning, He awakens My ear to hear as the learned.* ~Isaiah 50:4

> *Surely you have instructed many, and you have strengthened weak hands. Your words have upheld him who was stumbling, and you have strengthened the feeble knees.* ~Job 4:3-4

> *Pleasant words are like a honeycomb, Sweetness to the soul and health to the bones.*
> ~Proverbs 16:24

Dick Mills knew nothing about me. God showed him my future preaching and teaching ministry. He told me that my words would bring healing to the broken hearted and hope to many. He also said that my words spoken under the anointing of the Holy Spirit would bring physical healing to the hearers.

Another revelation about the hummingbird is in its name. It's called a hummingbird. My wife and I are very musical. We play instruments and lead worship. From the time I gave my life to the Lord in 1981 until today I've been in a Christian Band or on a worship team playing drums or guitar. My daughters are also gifted musicians and singers.

I don't think every time I see a bird that God is trying to speak to me, but there are times when we need to be aware and alert. Just knowing that God can speak though nature can open opportunities to hear something unique and profound from God. Who knows how many times God has tried to say something to you through nature and you were unaware?

One January I was visiting a church when the pastor shared an experience he had that morning. He was looking at his snow covered back yard and eight Turtle Doves (sometimes called Mourning Doves) were walking around picking at the snow. The number eight in Biblical Numerology is the number of new beginnings. As he considered the eight doves in his back yard God spoke to his heart that this new year was going be a year of new beginnings, and that there would be a fresh blessing and anointing of the Holy Spirit to do new ministry. It was just one month later that God reassigned me to a new church to pastor. With the new assignment came a fresh new anointing and grace.

GOD SPEAKS IN MANY WAYS

For God may speak in one way, or in another,
Yet man does not perceive it. ~Job 33:14

Everything that God communicates to us will never contradict the Bible. It will never undermine God's character as revealed in the Bible.

My wife and I like to walk around in the mall from time to time. Sometimes for no purpose except to window shop, talk and enjoy the atmosphere. We were walking past a shoe store with very cool displays and we decided to go in and try on some shoes. The salesman and I got along really well; I usually like people who laugh at my jokes. Suddenly the salesman switched gears and started to prophecy to me by predicting an event that would happen to me in the upcoming summer.

I immediately felt a check in my spirit but patiently listened to him so I could discern what was happening. When he was done with his predictions he never gave glory to God. The character of the predictions did not encourage me in my walk with God at all. Then he told me things about myself that he could not have possibly known except by some supernatural source. This is when I told him to stop. This man was not a prophetic person moving in the true Spirit of God; this guy was a psychic, trafficking with demons. I tried to talk to him about Jesus and the true nature of prophecy from God. True prophecy from God strengthens people in their walk with God, builds them up and brings glory to God. He would not get right with God but insisted that his psychic ability was from God and that he knew Jesus.

We must reach a level of maturity where we can easily recognize when God is speaking and when He is not. When you know His ways and character by your knowledge of the Bible and years of relationship, discernment is not difficult. If someone told me something my wife had said to them, I would almost immediately know if they were telling the truth. I know my wife so well that I can pretty much predict how she will react and what she would say in almost any situation. While the God of the Bible can be much more mysterious, he still acts within the boundaries of His character as revealed in the Bible.

> *And when they say to you, "Seek those who are mediums and wizards, who whisper and mutter, should not a people seek their God? Should they seek the dead on behalf of the living? To the law and to the testimony! If they do not speak according to this word, it is because there is no light in them. They will pass through it hard-pressed and hungry; and it shall happen, when they are hungry, that they will be enraged and curse their king and their God, and look upward. Then they will look to the earth, and see trouble and darkness, gloom of anguish; and they will be driven into darkness."* ~Isaiah 8:19-22

SPIRIT WORLD

The last part of the above quotation from scripture states that those who listen to psychics, trans-channelers/mediums and wizards will be driven into trouble, gloom and darkness. If you look to sources of supernatural knowledge that are not of God you are opening yourself up to great deception and delusion.

Besides measuring supernatural experience by the revealed character of God, we will also find times when things are in direct contradiction to scripture passages.

I was chaperoning a trip to Chicago for my daughter's high school choir. On the bus I got into a conversation with a middle-aged man who was an excellent guitar player. He had backed up the choir in some pop music performances and could play famous riffs note for note. Through our conversation he found out that I was a Pentecostal Pastor (Pentecostals believe that tongues and the prophetic gifts of the Holy Spirit are for today; see 1 Corinthians 12:7-11). He told me that he was once a Pentecostal and prayed in tongues often (tongues are a heavenly language not learned by natural means; see Acts 2:4). One day he was driving in his car and praying in tongues when he heard a voice tell him to STOP praying in tongues. The voice was so emphatic that he concluded that it must be God. From that day forward he never spoke in tongues again. He then asked me what my opinion was of that experience. I told him that the voice he heard could not possibly be of God because God is not going to tell him something that is in direct contradiction to His Word. I showed him the following scripture:

> *Therefore, brethren, desire earnestly to prophesy, and do not forbid to speak with tongues.* ~1 Corinthians 14:39

After being confronted with a clear Bible verse that contradicted his experience, his reaction baffled me. He told me it didn't matter what the Bible said because he heard a clear audible command from God and was never going to speak in tongues again. He was very stubborn about it. I tried to explain to him that when voices or angelic visitations contradict the Bible, we must always obey the Bible. The Bible has the final authority and say on what we believe and practice. I then pointed out to him a personal favorite Bible verse that's just before 1 Corinthians 14:39; it's verse 38 – *"But if anyone is ignorant, let him be ignorant."*

God does speak in more ways than we realize. *"For God may speak in one way, or in another, yet man does not perceive it" (Job 33:14).* Let's go to the Bible and discover what believers in the New Testament experienced. Consider all the ways that God spoke in the Book of Acts alone:

- Angels spoke to the disciples – Acts 1:10-11, 5:19-20, 8:26
- Through anointed preaching – Acts 2:14-40
- The audible voice of God – Acts 9:5-7
- Visions – Acts 9:10-13, 10:3-5, 26:19
- Signs and wonders – Acts 8:13, 13:9-12
- Through dreams and visions of the night – Acts 16:9, 18:9-10
- The prophetic ministry – Acts 11:28, 15:32
- Common sense and knowledge of the Scripture – Acts 13:46-47
- Circumstance and common sense – Acts 14:4-7
- Witness of the Holy Spirit and inner peace – Acts 15:28, 34
- Lack of peace, or constrained by the Holy Spirit – Acts 16:6-7
- Provoked, compelled or stirred within by the Holy Spirit – Acts 17:16, 18:5
- Personal visitation of the Lord – Acts 23:11

SPIRIT WORLD

God, who at various times and in various ways spoke in time past to the fathers by the prophets, has in these last days spoken to us by His Son, whom He has appointed heir of all things, through whom also He made the worlds.

~Hebrews 1:1-2

God truly has spoken in various ways and times. Although the avenues that God uses to communicate are diverse, there is a foundation to hearing clearly. That foundation is the Word of God. What God says will always match His word and character as revealed in the Bible.

In the next couple of chapters we will discuss the still small voice of God, how to develop your ability to hear God better, and how God speaks through the Word of God. If you have God in a box I pray that He would shatter it. No matter how ornate the box is, it's still a box. God will not be contained. In the C. S. Lewis classic book series, "The Chronicles of Narnia", Aslan is the majestic lion king that is a powerful force for good. The Narnians often say, "He's not a tame lion." Jesus is unquestionably good, but He's not a tame lion.

Chapter 3

THE STILL SMALL VOICE

My sheep hear My voice, and I know them, and they follow Me. ~John 10:27

Everyone hears the voice of God to some extent, especially His sheep. The clarion call of God has gone out into all the world, the Holy Spirit bearing witness that Jesus is the Christ (see Romans 10:18). Our problem is that we fail to recognize the voice of God. Amongst all the cacophony of endless babble inside our heads and coming from the world, the voice of God can easily be dismissed. Strong holds of false beliefs cause us to reject the Holy Spirit bearing witness to the truth. A seared conscience cannot feel the prick of righteous conviction. It is a scary thing to be so delusional in your mind and so scarred in your conscience that you cannot hear God anymore. When God calls, the automated voice on the phone says, "This line has been disconnected and is no longer in service." How can we recognize the voice of God better and maintain a tender heart so that we continually hear? I'm glad you asked.

SPIRIT WORLD

When I turned sixteen years old my Father bought me a junker car. It was a 1964 Chevrolet Biscayne with four doors and a lot of rust to hold it together. It only cost him $75 but to me it was FREEDOM! It was built like a tank so my Dad didn't have to worry about me surviving my first Michigan winter on slippery roads. After the first ice and snow storm Dad made me drive him out to the High School parking lot to do some donuts (spinning the car around in a 360-degree circle) and some fishtails. He wanted me to get used to driving on icy slippery roads so he had me drive 35 miles-per-hour in a straight line and then crank the wheel. This would result in the car spinning around on the snow. He would then make me drive in a straight line and then begin turning the wheel left and right until the car fishtailed across the parking lot. Then he would say in a calm voice, "Take your foot off the gas and do not hit the brake, and then as the back end of the car spins left, turn your wheel slightly to the left. As the car spins right, turn the steering wheel right and eventually you will pull out of the fishtail." Thank God for Dad's tutelage, that first winter I only crashed into three ditches setting a new family record for first-time winter drivers. It was quite clear why my father invested only $75 in my first car. I can still hear him say, "Don't think you're ever going to drive my car."

Whenever I accidently went into a fishtail on an icy road I could hear his voice in my head telling me to be calm, take my foot off of the brake and slightly turn into the slide. Those words of wisdom probably saved my life a few times. This is similar to hearing our Heavenly Father's instructions. When we read our Bible we are putting the commands of God in our heart. We must hear things over and over, hearing them orally and in excess for them to take a firm root in our life. When trouble comes we will hear the wise instruction of the Word of God rise up from our spirit. The Holy Spirit will bring the Word of God that we have placed in our hearts to remembrance.

> *My son, keep your father's command,*
> *And do not forsake the law of your mother.*
> *Bind them continually upon your heart;*
> *Tie them around your neck.*
> *When you roam, they will lead you;*
> *When you sleep, they will keep you;*
> *And when you awake, they will speak with you.*
> *For the commandment is a lamp,*
> *And the law a light. Reproofs of instruction are*
> *the way of life.* ~Proverbs 6:20-23

One of the first things I did after possessing my $75 Chevrolet Biscayne was to go down to the car stereo shop and purchase a $250 stereo system. This was in 1976 so I'm sure it would be comparable to a $1000 car stereo system today. It had a cassette player instead of an eight-track player, which was going the way of the dinosaur. It had a 250-watt amplifier and two huge speakers that we mounted in the back window dash. We used the empty spacious trunk as a speaker box and the sound inside the car was incredible; it could make your ears bleed. We had several cliché sayings. One was, "If it's too loud, you're too old." Another was, "It's not the car you drive, it's the stereo inside." And last but not least, "Death to Disco!" Disco music was not allowed to defile the temple of classic rock that was my vehicle.

A couple of music lover friends and I would play this game where you focused on a single instrument in a song instead of just listening to the song as a whole. We got so good at this that we could hear just the drum and percussion parts, just the bass guitar part, or just the rhythm guitar. I started to get the hint that it wasn't normal when I would comment to a friend riding in my car, "Did you hear how cool that rhythm guitar part was in that section of the song?" And he would reply, "No I couldn't hear that, I'm just enjoying the song." In the same way that you can single out musical parts in a song you can also learn to single out the voice of God and develop your ability to hear from God through the disharmony in your heart.

Now fast forward to the 1990's when I was a youth pastor. Car stereos were taken to a whole new level of ear splitting brutality. This kid in my youth group had a 1200-watt amp in his car and huge bass speakers. When he pulled up to the church building the walls would shake and rattle from the concussive bass blasts. I would watch him exit his car to see if he would act like a punch drunk boxer. He had a sticker on his back bumper that read, "I do what the voices in my head tell me." That sticker was humorous and spooky at the same time. We definitely wanted this kid to distinguish between voices.

When I did youth ministry I would sometimes host youth rallies. At one small rally we had about 35 kids between the ages of twelve to eighteen. Because the theme of this rally was about listening to God and being obedient I opened it with a crazy crowd breaker. Some naïve young man would have to volunteer. After selecting the perfect victim (one whose parents wouldn't file a law suit if things went wrong), I had a couple of youth leaders blindfold him in the back room and had him remove his shoes and socks. After the youth leaders were convinced that he couldn't see a thing they led him to the front of the church. There was ample open space between the first row of chairs and the platform with a pulpit and musical instruments. As he stood on one end of this open space in front of his curious peers, I began to give him instructions.

"I am going to lead you with my voice to the other side of the church. You can only do what my voice tells you to do. You cannot listen to any other voice. Do not make a move without listening to my instructions.

Nod if you can understand." He nodded. "In front of you on the floor I have placed several rat traps. These are bigger than mouse traps and can break your toes." Upon hearing this, he curled up his big pink toes. I gave the command for everyone else to start yelling orders at him. It was a crazy scene. Some of the more sadistic boys in the youth group were hoping he would put his toes in one of the rat traps. The amazing thing was I didn't raise my voice to get his attention. I spoke just above normal volume and guided him successfully through the perilous maze of toe crunching traps. We proved it was possible to focus on one voice in a menagerie of crowded confusion.

Whether you turn to the right or to the left, your ears will hear a voice behind you, saying, "This is the way; walk in it."
~Isaiah 30:21 NIV

TO BECOME A CHRISTIAN YOU MUST HEAR FROM GOD

No one can come to Me unless the Father who sent Me draws him; and I will raise him up at the last day. It is written in the prophets, 'And they shall all be taught by God.' Therefore everyone who has heard and learned from the Father comes to Me. *~John 6:44-45*

Before you even begin your Christian journey you hear the voice of God. A deep longing and yearning draws you to the Creator. There isn't a Christian on the planet that can say that they have not heard from God. To become a Born Again Christian you must yield to the inner call. It is a spiritual call; deep calls unto deep. It's first heard in the heart and then in the head. Spiritual impressions translate into thoughts. For most people, the voice of God does not come in a ticker tape of words that are read in your mind's eye, they come as an impression, a knowing, and a witness.

When you are about to make a bad choice that you know is wrong, there is an impression in your spirit that convicts you with a warning: *"This is going to get you in trouble."* Or worse, the inner voice of your conscience speaks: *"Don't do this; you are going to really hurt somebody."* When you do the right thing, you sense the pleasure of God. It's God saying "Well done, good job."

The Spirit of God will also bear witness with your spirit that you are a child of God. You can know that you are saved and going to heaven. You don't have to guess, you can know now by the inner witness of the Spirit.

Romans 8:15-16 tell us *"For you did not receive the spirit of bondage again to fear, but you received the Spirit of adoption by whom we cry out, 'Abba, Father'. The Spirit Himself bears witness with our spirit that we are children of God."*

This inner witness is the basic level at which everyone hears from God. Sometimes a Christian will say, "I heard God speak to me today that I am on the right track. He told me that everything will be all right." They don't always mean that they heard inner audible words; they mean that they received a witness in their heart. God impressed upon them that everything will be all right. Hearing an inner audible voice would be a higher level of revelation. At times the inner witness is so strong that it's like an inner audible voice. I believe this is how the prophets of old heard the voice of God. A higher revelation than the inner audible voice would be an audible voice. The higher the level of revelation, the rarer the occurrence. As far as the voice of God is concerned, there are three levels:

1. The inner witness, impression, conscience, intuition, or knowing
2. The inner audible voice
3. The audible voice of God

Hearing the audible voice of God is not a normal Christian experience. It is rare. There are several incidents in the New Testament of Jesus and the disciples hearing the audible voice of God (see Matthew 3:17, 17:5 and John 12:28-29).

A CALL TO MINISTRY

I heard the audible voice of God when I was called into the ministry. I realize that not everyone has been graced with this kind of an experience, and just because a person did not have a dramatic audible voice confirming his or her call to ministry does not mean their call is any less legitimate. A strong knowing in your heart that you are called to ministry is just as valid. If someone tells me they feel a call to ministry I don't discourage them. Who am I to say whether they heard from God or not. The fruit, or outward evidence of that call, will be the ultimate sign as to whether someone heard from God. A person who displays a true call to ministry will have a servant's heart and will find outlets to minister.

I went through a very discouraging time as a young Christian. After repeating the sinner's prayer at an altar and becoming "born again", I joined a Christian Rock band and we played at Jesus Festivals, churches, and Coffee shops. We even recorded our own album. It was an exciting time ministering to folks and sharing my faith. The band broke up and I went from signing autographs to slinging hash at a local truck stop/family restaurant. I would come home from work to my lonely rented house and wonder, "What now? What am I supposed to do now? I thought this band was going to fulfill my dreams of becoming a professional musician."

One day I came home late in the evening and began walking upstairs to my loft and bedroom. As I trudged up the stairs I heard the audible voice of God say, *"Feed My sheep."* I knew it was the voice of God! It came from all around me and inside of me at the same time; God's voice was Omni-directional. I went to my bedroom, prayed in the Spirit (praying in tongues) and worshiped for a while contemplating what this all meant. Was God calling me to teach the Bible? Did he want me to pastor a church?

The next evening I came home late, and as I ascended up the stairs to my loft God spoke audibly again! *"Feed My sheep."* Again, I prayed and worshiped for a while before going to sleep. The next evening, I came home and stopped just before climbing my stairs. "What would happen? Would God speak again?" As I approached the halfway mark, God spoke audibly the third and final time; He said, *"Feed My lambs."* As I knelt down to worship He spoke in an inner audible voice. This was much stronger than an inner witness. The Holy Spirit told me that I was to prepare myself for full-time ministry. He even told me what college to attend and begin my training. It was at this Bible training institute that I met my wife to be.

In time I understood why I needed an audible voice and others did not. First of all, I was not obvious ministry material. I would swish my shoulder length hair back and relate to my friends how I heard the audible voice of God calling me into ministry; snickers, snorts and belly laughs would result.

"Man, I don't know what you heard but maybe that was a flash back from all the LSD you took before you became a Christian," one friend theorized.

The Still Small Voice

"I cannot see you as a minister. You are not the type. You're not serious enough. In fact, you're down right goofy." This seemed to be the general consensus. Apparently, the stereotypical preacher is so stone sober that his very presence sucks all joy from the room.

I know what God told me. I could not deny it. I obeyed the audible voice of God. I began teaching the Bible whenever and wherever I could. I taught bible studies in my home. I taught the youth group at my church. I went to the jails, prisons, and assisted living homes. I pretty much taught in every socially acceptable and non-socially-acceptable genre that I could. The amazing thing about it was that God used me. Folks young and old would say, "Your teaching really feeds me." Apparently when I heard the audible voice of God an impartation/ability to teach and preach the Bible came into me. It was apparent to me that God can use whomever He wants. A divine call of God is not up for a vote. Either you are called or you're not. I love what Paul states at the beginning of many of his letters, *"Paul, an apostle not from men nor through man, but through Jesus Christ and God the Father who raised Him from the dead" (Galatians 1:1).*

THE FOUNDATION OF THE CHURCH IS BUILT ON PERSONALLY HEARING FROM GOD

Simon Peter answered and said, "You are the Christ, the Son of the living God." Jesus answered and said to him, "Blessed are you, Simon Bar-Jonah, for flesh and blood has not revealed this to you, but My Father who is in heaven. And I also say to you that you are Peter, and on this rock I will build My church, and the gates of Hades shall not prevail against it.
~Matthew 16:16-18

Peter received a revelation that Jesus was the Christ, the Son of the living God. Flesh and blood did not reveal this to him. He received a personal revelation from God. The rock on which Jesus builds His church is not Peter; it's the rock of personal revelation that Jesus is the Christ! The church of the living God is built on human beings having personal encounters with God. To become a Christian, you must receive a personal revelation from the Father that Jesus is the Christ, the Son of the living God. If you are a Christian believer, you cannot say that you do not hear from God. You must have heard from Him at least once, when you came to believe with all your heart that Jesus is the Christ.

Peter cannot be the rock on which the church was built because the church was built on the chief cornerstone, which is Christ (see Ephesians 2:20). *"No other foundation can anyone lay than that which is laid, which is Jesus Christ" (1 Corinthians 3:11).* When a person's faith is built on an authentic God encounter, on a very personal revelation and surrender to the truth of the Gospel, they will not easily deny Christ.

In ancient times the city fathers would gather at the gate of the city to have council and make pronouncements. Contracts between people were ratified. Major decisions were debated and deliberated. When Jesus said that the gates of hell would not prevail against His church, He meant that the councils of hell itself would not be diabolical and conniving enough to destroy the church. A church built on Jesus and personal encounters with Him will survive the onslaughts of hell. Your personal faith built on the reality of Christ will not be easily shaken by tricky deceptions and false arguments. **"A man with an experience of God is never at the mercy of a man with an argument."** (Leonard Ravenhill). A spiritual experience with God is more real than life itself.

> Because Your loving kindness is better than life,
> My lips shall praise You.
> Thus I will bless You while I live;
> I will lift up my hands in Your name.

My soul shall be satisfied as with marrow and fatness,
And my mouth shall praise You with joyful lips.   ~Psalm 63:3-5

FOLLOWING THE PEACE OF GOD

For you shall go out with joy,
And be led out with peace;
The mountains and the hills
Shall break forth into singing before you,
And all the trees of the field shall clap their hands.
~Isaiah 55:12

Being led by the peace of God can be a tricky thing because we have a sinful nature to deal with. We must learn to discern between the false peace of convenience and the true peace of God. If you experience some major conflict at your place of employment you may become exasperated and quit. This may offer some temporary relief but then you run out of money and your car gets repossessed. Before quitting a perfectly good job, shouldn't you at least pray and search your heart for God's peace and direction. My Dad used to say, "Don't quit a job until you have another one." Sound wisdom. Just doing what we feel like at any given moment is not the same as following the peace of God. Sometimes God will deliver us FROM a situation, and sometimes He will deliver us THROUGH a situation.

A person may be having an ongoing argument with their spouse, and then after packing up and leaving they have a temporary peace. Why? Because they're out of the conflict. Relief from a stressful situation is not the same as the inner peace of God. It would be so much easier to just walk away and avoid all potential conflict than to try and work it out. The true peace of God may go contrary to what YOU want to do.

SPIRIT WORLD

The peace of God will always be on the side of righteousness; not always on the side of convenience.

The Word of God promises us that peace can be found in tumultuous circumstances. In the Kingdom of God there is peace. *"For the kingdom of God is not eating and drinking, but righteousness and peace and joy in the Holy Spirit" (Romans 14:17).* In this world we may be having tribulation, but in the Holy Spirit there is peace. Picture a circle on the ground; the moment you step inside that circle you have tremendous peace. When you step outside of it there is unbelievable stress, fear and anxiety. Inside the circle your stressful situation is still present, but it's just outside the circle. Stepping inside the circle is like staying in the Spirit. It's like being in a state where you are constantly being filled with the Spirit. In the Holy Spirit there is righteousness, peace and joy no matter what is going on in your life outside that circle. We need to step into the Holy Spirit at all times; being filled with the Spirit, walking in the Spirit, and being led by the Spirit of Peace.

> *And let the peace of God **rule in your hearts**, to which also you were called in one body; and be thankful.* ~Colossians 3:15

> *And let the peace (soul harmony which comes) from Christ rule **(act as umpire continually)** in your hearts [deciding and settling with finality all questions that arise in your minds, in that peaceful state] to which as [members of Christ's] one body you were also called [to live]. And be thankful (appreciative), [giving praise to God always].* ~Colossians 3:15 AMP

Notice that the peace of God is to rule in our hearts. I like the way the Amplified translation puts it, "acts as umpire continually." In the same way that an umpire calls the plays on the baseball field, so God's peace can help us find the right path. Have you ever heard another Christian say, "I just don't have a peace about that"? Or they might say something

The Still Small Voice

like, "I am getting a check in my spirit." When Christians say things like this it's because God is nudging them not to do something or to think a decision through a little more.

There is a good story in the Old Testament about a King who acted compulsively and didn't wait for God's peace. In the book of 1 Samuel 13, King Saul saw that he was outnumbered by the enemy and that his men would not fight until Samuel the prophet came and offered a sacrifice beseeching God's protection and favor. Samuel was running late and many of Saul's men were deserting out of fear. The enemy forces kept increasing while King Saul's army was decreasing. It didn't take a genius to figure out that the longer they waited the more the odds were against them for victory. King Saul broke God's law by offering the sacrifice that could only be offered by the priest/prophet. Just as Saul finished the sacrifice Samuel arrived and rebuked him for his arrogance and lack of faith. The prophet told him that God was about to bring a miraculous victory and exult him in a major way, but eventually he would lose his kingdom to someone more worthy. That "someone" turned out to be David. King Saul responded in a way that brings us great insight into how we are pushed into bad decisions.

> *And Samuel said, "What have you done?" Saul said, "When I saw that the people were scattered from me, and that you did not come within the days appointed, and that the Philistines gathered together at Michmash, then I said, 'The Philistines will now come down on me at Gilgal, and I have not made supplication to the LORD.' Therefore I **felt compelled**, and offered a burnt offering."*   ~1 Samuel 13:11-12

How many times have you made decisions out of stress, fear and compulsion rather than searching inwardly for the peace of God? If the enemy of our souls, the devil, can push you through fearfulness he will. A major breakthrough could be right around the corner but if you jump

SPIRIT WORLD

ahead of God it could spoil the promotion. If you don't have a peace, refuse to be pushed. I will be led by the Lord, but I will not be pushed by the devil.

> *Wait on the LORD;*
> *Be of good courage,*
> *And He shall strengthen your heart;*
> *Wait, I say, on the LORD!* ~Psalm 27:14
>
> *Depart from evil and do good;*
> *Seek peace and pursue it.* ~Psalm 34:14

When I was about to graduate from a Bible institute, (my first two years of Bible college), I was doing an internship at a great church in St. Charles, Michigan. I discovered that there was a prayer meeting on a weekday morning and I asked the Pastor if I could attend. He said, "Well, you're welcome to but it's some of our older matronly women of the church." I expressed that I wanted to learn more about intercession and it didn't matter to me who attended as long as they knew how to pray. He kinda chuckled and said, "Oh, you'll learn a few things all right."

The morning finally came and I knocked on the classroom door where the prayer meeting was being held. "Come on in young preacher." The voice was definitely matronly, and when I stepped in the ladies were sitting in a circle around the perimeter of the small classroom. The woman leading the group mentioned that they should pray for a woman in the church who was in poor health. Fervent praying in tongues broke out as some began rocking slightly forward and back with their eyes closed tight. They would take turns crying out to God in English for healing and a total recovery. This went on for ten or fifteen minutes until there was a breakthrough followed by total peace. Everyone stopped praying in tongues and after a minute they would begin all over again with another prayer burden. This process reminded me of kayaking down a river where there were rapids and then a slow peaceful lazy flow of the river until you came to another stretch of rapids.

I finally spoke up in the meeting and asked a question, "What is going on?" The leader of the pack of grey-top prayer warriors said, "Son, what kind of Pentecostal preacher are you? Haven't you ever learned to pray through?"

"Pray through to what?"

"Pray though to the PEACE!" "We pray until God lifts the burden. Sometimes we have to keep praying for something week after week until we feel we've prayed through."

WOW! I never knew there was such a thing as praying through. **Sometimes we pray the prayer of faith, believing it is done, and most of the time we need to pray through to the peace.**

> *Be anxious for nothing, but in everything by prayer and supplication, with thanksgiving, let your requests be made known to God; and the peace of God, which surpasses all understanding, will guard your hearts and minds through Christ Jesus.* ~Philippians 4:6-7

The cure for an anxious mind is praying through to the peace of God. When you get to that peace, it puts a guard around heart (emotional state) and mind (thoughts). This is not ordinary peace. This is a peace that surpasses all understanding. This is the peace from God Himself. How the world longs for a little peace. Folks spend millions of dollars for a temporary escape from their anxious thoughts and feelings. True inner peace can only be found in blissful communion with the Spirit of the living God.

THE STILL SMALL VOICE

Then He said, "Go out, and stand on the mountain before the LORD." And behold, the LORD passed by, and a great and strong wind tore into the mountains and broke the rocks in pieces before the LORD, but the LORD was not in the wind; and after the wind an earthquake, but the LORD was not in the earthquake; and after the earthquake a fire, but the LORD was not in the fire; and after the fire a still small voice (emphasis mine). ~1 Kings 19:11-12

Some folks are always looking for God to speak or confirm something to them in a big dramatic way; a raging wind, the earth and mountains shaking, or a fire ball from heaven. Because they are looking for this huge experience, they miss the subtle witness of the Spirit. God's voice is constant. A steady stream of peace and stability. God is speaking in a still small voice but we have to quiet ourselves to listen. Look inward to where the Holy Spirit resides in your spirit and you will know what God is saying. You do hear from God; we have established that.

My sheep hear My voice, and I know them, and they follow Me. ~John 10:27

As a pastor of a great church, I am responsible to hear from God about what to preach and teach on Sunday mornings. Sometimes the weight of the responsibility can seem overwhelming. People are coming to church to hear a word from God. They need inspiration and encouragement. They need to feel the love and challenge of the Word and the Holy Spirit. There will be visitors who don't know Jesus. This may be the only time they have ever dared grace the door of a church. There will be first-time visitors who have become disenfranchised from any church or "organized religion." This Sunday could be the last chance for the church to connect with them.

We have a Thursday evening prayer meeting at our church. This is where I wait on God to give confirmation to me about what I am to preach on. I may currently be in the middle of preaching a series, but I never assume that the Lord wants me to stay on a particular subject. I like to check in with Him to get confirmation. During the prayer time, I remain open to the Spirit. After all, it's God's church, I don't tell Him what His people need; He tells me. I have been in a series of messages and God has impressed upon me to share something off subject and unrelated to the series. Afterwards, I resume the series.

There have been times when I wrestle with a message. A subject will persist in my mind and spirit but I may not feel comfortable with it. One week I felt strongly that I was to share what the Bible had to say about homosexuality, and I didn't want to teach this message. I felt intimidated and wasn't sure it would come out loving enough. I thought for sure that folks knew what the New Testament says about this touchy subject; that the Bible is crystal clear that homosexuality is sin, and a heaven or hell issue (see Romans 1:24-27 and 1 Corinthians 6:9-11). I just didn't want to do it. But the witness of the Spirit was so strong. I tried to ignore the still small consistent voice of God, but I became frustrated. I had no peace until I surrendered to God.

You have to understand, I can put sermon notes together in my sleep. I can pick any subject and put a teaching together about it. This ability is a gift from God. It would be easy for me to teach what I want and ignore God, but I also know that disobedience has consequences. I don't always know what they will be, but I hate missing God. I love my heavenly Father and want to please Him. I want to be faithful to the sacred trust of teaching His people the Word of God.

It was during one of our Thursday evening prayer meetings that, after much personal deliberation with God, I found peace in sharing the

SPIRIT WORLD

message that God wanted me to preach on homosexuality. I had to pray through to the peace. God's people need constant affirmation on right and wrong. The world muddies issues to where even the most discerning individual is blinded by grey. Right will always be right, and wrong will always be wrong. As long as we can share the truth with love we should not be intimidated. We should be able to share the wrong of an issue and exude a genuine concern. The bottom line is that sin hurts people. And if we truly love people, we will reach deep inside and pull out the courage to throw them a rope of truth and rescue them from sinking in a quicksand of deception. I taught that message on homosexuality and had many people thank me for helping them see clearly what the Word of God said about such a hot button subject in a politically correct landscape. Many of our teenagers go through what I call a "gender identity crisis" because no one has the courage to tell them what is right and wrong for fear of being labeled a bigot. When all voices are silenced that declare something is wrong and displeases God, and all you hear are affirmations to follow your every feeling, the boundaries of conscience begin to fade. When we know what pleases our heavenly Father and what is clearly sin, we can resist temptation. We can take captive every vain thought, and bring it into obedience to Christ and His Word.

There have been several times that God has instructed me to preach hard messages and I wrestled with Him. It's hard to hear from God clearly when you're fighting Him. If you will wait on Him, take time to listen to the still small voice, you will know the will of God. You must desire His will more than your own. You must pray through to the peace of God. Sometimes it depends on how badly you want your will, or God's will.

> *If any man desires to do His will (God's pleasure), he will know (have the needed illumination to recognize and can tell for*

himself) whether the teaching is from God or whether I am speaking from Myself and of My own accord and on My own authority. He who speaks on his own authority seeks to win honor for himself. [He whose teaching originates with himself seeks his own glory.] But He Who seeks the glory and is eager for the honor of Him Who sent Him, He is true; and there is no unrighteousness or falsehood or deception in Him.
~John 7:17-18 AMP

IF YOU ARE OBEDIENT TO WHAT YOU KNOW MORE WILL BE GIVEN

Then He said to them, "Take heed what you hear. With the same measure you use, it will be measured to you; and to you who hear, more will be given. For whoever has, to him more will be given; but whoever does not have, even what he has will be taken away from him." ~Mark 4:24-25

If we are obedient to the truth we know, and the light we have been given, more will be given us. If we are diligent to search for God's will and obey it, more illumination will light our path.

When I worked as a short order cook in a truck stop/family restaurant, I was having a discussion with one of the other cooks about hearing from God. The dishwasher was listening in and suddenly came out of her work area and blurted out, "I want to hear from God!" What do I have to do to hear from God?" I took her back into her dish area so that no one could hear us, and then I told her, "God is speaking to you right now. In fact, He's been speaking to you for some time. Do you want to know what He has been saying?"

"Of course I want to know what He's saying."

"He's telling you to turn to Jesus. He shed His blood on the cross so you could be forgiven of your sins. He is waiting for you to ask Him to

SPIRIT WORLD

forgive you. I can lead you in a prayer right now and you can surrender your life to Christ making Him your personal Lord and Savior. If you are willing to turn from what you know is wrong, He will come into your heart and change your life. Can you hear Him speaking to you right now? The Holy Spirit is bearing witness to the truth. Can you feel the tug of God on your heart? You can be born again into a whole new life."

We stood there looking at each other for a moment until she lowered her eyes and said that she didn't want to turn her life over to Jesus right then. I asked, "Why? I know you are hearing Him talk to you and that you feel the pull of His love. Why won't you listen to Him?" She told me that she was afraid of being a hypocrite. I explained to her that she doesn't have to be a hypocrite. She could be a shining example of a Christian. She just has to have a sincere heart. She persisted in resisting God so I had no choice but to relent. I left the conversation by explaining to her that until she obeyed what God was telling her right then, she would not grow in hearing from Him.

What is the last thing God told you to do? Have you been obedient? Has God been laying something on your heart over a long period of time? Are you are finding it hard to obey His still small voice? You must move forward in the things He is putting on your heart. We must become more diligent to obey.

Most Christians want to know the will of God for their life. They have a sense of destiny but don't know where to start. Sometimes He does not give you the full ten-year plan. He will only shine light on the path right in front of you. As you are faithful in the baby steps forward, then He will give you more. More vision comes to those who are faithful with the small things.

> *But the path of the just is like the shining sun,*
> *That shines ever brighter unto the perfect day.* ~Proverbs 4:18

The Still Small Voice

Follow the Lord today and more light will be given you. You and I can't see clearly into the future. We have to trust God. Don't let fear of what may lie ahead rob you of joy today. As we obey what we know today, more light will be given us tomorrow.

> *But seek first the kingdom of God and His righteousness, and all these things shall be added to you. Therefore do not worry about tomorrow, for tomorrow will worry about its own things. Sufficient for the day is its own trouble.* ~Matthew 6:33-34

*Declare the Word of God to any situation
and watch it line up.
Don't be impatient; persevere to the harvest.*

Chapter 4

GOD'S WORD IS SPIRIT AND LIFE

It is the Spirit who gives life; the flesh profits nothing. The words that I speak to you are spirit, and they are life.
~John 6:63

For prophecy never had its origin in the will of man, but men spoke from God as they were carried along by the Holy Spirit.
~2 Peter 1:21 NIV

The Bible is more than the words of men; it is the Word of God. It has a supernatural source and therefore has spiritual force. The Word of God rings true in the deepest part of man, it goes past emotions and intellect to the spiritual core. Because the source of the Bible is the Spirit of God, the fountainhead of all creation, healing and the primal essence of life are infused in its syntax. Man's spirit perks up and gives attention at the entrance of God's Word. Never underestimate the power of God's word to convert the soul and make wise the simple (see Psalm 19:7).

SPIRIT WORLD

Jesus said that His words are spirit and life. When we take in God's Word we are ingesting vitality and the stuff that brings health to our whole being. In the same way that a doctor gives a prescription of medicine to restore health, God's word is medicine to the soul. It will bring life and vibrancy to your whole being.

> *My son, attend to my words; consent and submit to my sayings. Let them not depart from your sight; keep them in the center of your heart.* ***For they are life to those who find them, healing and health to all their flesh.***   *~Proverbs 4:20-22 AMP*

GOD'S WORD IS ALIVE AND ENERGIZING

> *For the word of God is living and powerful, and sharper than any two-edged sword, piercing even to the division of soul and spirit, and of joints and marrow, and is a discerner of the thoughts and intents of the heart.*   *~Hebrews 4:12*

There are two Greek words that are translated into the English word "life" in the Bible. The first is bios, from which we get the word biology, which is the study of living organisms. The second Greek word for life is zoe (Strong's #2222), which goes beyond the concept of physical life to spiritual life and a higher quality of life, it's the God kind of blessed life. Jesus said in John 10:10, *"I came to give life (zoe) more abundantly."* This is a super-abundant extraordinary life. It is experienced in this present life of grace and looks forward to a future life of glory. The Word of God has this kind of life in it; God's Word imparts zoe life to its reader.

> *The Word of God is alive and powerful. The Greek word for powerful is energes (Strong's #1756), which is one of the energy words of the Bible. The Word of God is active and energizing. It's working in you! For this reason we also thank God without ceasing, because when you received the word of God which you heard from us, you welcomed it not as the*

word of men, but as it is in truth, the word of God, which also effectively works in you who believe.   ~1 Thessalonians 2:13

In the above verse, the Word of God **effectively works** in you who believe. This is another one of the energy words, energeo (Strong's #1754). There have been times I have read my Bible and literally felt life and energy infusing into me. Never underestimate the faith, hope and love the living Word can bring to your soul. If there ever was a time we needed fresh hope it's now. There are so many things in life that are trying to steal hope and bring despondency. The living promises of God's Word are speaking life and hope to you. God's word is not dead ink, it's alive! Jesus said that the words that He speaks are spirit and life.

All Scripture is given by inspiration of God, and is profitable for doctrine, for reproof, for correction, for instruction in righteousness, that the man of God may be complete, thoroughly equipped for every good work.   ~2 Timothy 3:16-17

The Greek word for "given by the inspiration of God" is theopneustos, which literally means "God breathed." The gusto and vigor of God Almighty is infused in His letter to us. We need to approach the Bible with faith that God can bring life, energy and healing through hearing His Word. God's word is spiritual and powerful.

GOD'S WORD IS INCORRUPTIBLE SEED

Having been born again, not of corruptible seed but incorruptible, through the word of God which lives and abides forever.   ~1 Peter 1:23

So the word of the Lord grew mightily and prevailed.   ~Acts 19:20

SPIRIT WORLD

One of my first jobs was to wash dishes at a local restaurant. I was sixteen and cocky. During the rush hours they had to pair us up, and even with two people working it was sometimes a challenge to clean and cycle the dishes fast enough to get them back to the server stations. Wouldn't you know that God, in His providence, paired me up with a radical born-again Christian man? He had a little Gideon's New Testament with Psalms and Proverbs tucked into his back pocket. He called it his witnessing dagger. I was completely fascinated with this guy in a sort of detached intellectual way. Much like the way an archeologist studies the religious artifacts of an ancient culture, I was trying to ascertain if he was nuts or the real thing. I had never met anyone so fired up about Jesus and the Bible before.

I was raised in a traditional Missouri Synod Lutheran Church. We didn't have fanatics in our church. Our mantra was, "All things in moderation." This included drinking alcoholic beverages, Pecan and Coconut Cream pie, and religion. The only person who quoted the Bible outside of my church was my mother, and she quoted things like, "Cleanliness is next to godliness" and "God helps those who help themselves." Imagine my surprise when I found out those verses weren't even in the Bible.

So here comes this Bible-quoting Jesus freak making me his personal evangelistic mission in life. In our little conversations about God and life he often had me against the ropes, jabbing convicting scriptures at me. Whenever he almost had me cornered to make a decision for Christ, I would lay down a magnificent smoke screen to avoid dealing with my many sins. I would ask things like, "What about the dinosaurs?" or "How do you reconcile evolution to the Bible?" et cetera, et cetera, et cetera...

One day as we worked he asked me why I believed I was going to heaven. I told him that all you have to do is believe Jesus is your savior and you will go to heaven, right? Then he decided to stop playing games with me and he let me have the Gospel with both guns-a-blazing.

He began his tirade with, "There are different levels of belief. In James 2:19 the Bible says, 'You believe there is one God. You do well. Even the demons believe—and tremble!' The Bible says that the demons believe. Do you think that because the demons believe they are going to heaven? Of course not. Therefore, there are different levels of belief. Just knowing something is true is not saving faith. You can have a mental assent to a historical fact like George Washington was the first president of the United States, or Jesus Christ died on a cross. But a mental assent is not saving faith. When Peter and the disciples believed that Jesus was the Christ they left ALL to follow Him. What have YOU given up to follow Jesus? Revelation 3:15-16 says, *"I know your works that you are neither cold nor hot. I wish you were cold or hot. So then, because you are lukewarm, and neither cold nor hot, I will vomit you out of My mouth."* A halfhearted commitment will not make it. If you're lukewarm in your commitment to Christ you are putrid to Him, He will spit you out of His mouth. That means you won't go to heaven. You will go to hell."

Wow! I was speechless (which is kind of a big deal with me). The Word of God penetrated my heart. I felt the impacting conviction but I refused to let my outward appearance show it. The truth of God's Word had located where I was living, I was lukewarm and not fully committed. I was believing a lie that I could just have faith in Jesus and then live any way I wanted to. I knew Jesus as my savior, but not as my Lord. The two-edged sword of the living Word had exposed the lie I was living.

> *For the word of God is living and powerful, and sharper than any two-edged sword, piercing even to the division of soul and spirit, and of joints and marrow, and is a discerner of the thoughts and intents of the heart.* ~Hebrews 4:12

SPIRIT WORLD

The reason I didn't want to show any conviction was because I wasn't sure I wanted to change my lifestyle. I wasn't sure I wanted to live for Jesus whole heartedly. I would forever be altered from that encounter because those words implanted themselves into my soul. The Word of God is called the incorruptible seed (see 1 Peter 1:23). The seed had been planted into my heart and there was no uprooting it. Every time I would go out partying with my friends I would hear in my spirit, "You are lukewarm, neither cold nor hot." The implanted Word tormented me for several years. The seed of God's word grew mightily and finally prevailed. In a time of personal crisis, I surrendered my life to Christ. I no longer wanted to live a lie. Such is the power of God's Word, it is spirit and life. God's word will accomplish what He sends it to do. It will not return void. Keep planting the Word of God in your heart and into the hearts of others and patiently wait for a harvest of righteousness.

> *For as the rain comes down, and the snow from heaven, and do not return there, but water the earth, and make it bring forth and bud, that it may give seed to the sower and bread to the eater, so shall My word be that goes forth from My mouth; It shall not return to Me void, but it shall accomplish what I please, and it shall prosper in the thing for which I sent it.*
> *~Isaiah 55:10-11*

What do you need? If you have a need, sow a seed. There are many of God's promises in the Bible that address every situation in life. If you are dealing with a lot of anger, there are verses that you can plant in your spirit about anger. "The wrath of man does not produce the righteousness of God" (James 1:20). There are plenty of verses in the book of Proverbs that deal with anger. Find these verses and read them out loud.

Plant these scriptures in your heart and they will grow, first the blade, then the head, and after that the full grain in the head. When the grain ripens then it's harvest time (see Mark 4:26-29). The Word of God will grow mightily and prevail over sin (see Acts 19:20).

What about worry? Will the seed of God's word grow mightily and prevail over worry? Yes, it will! Dr. Jesus is writing you a prescription for combating worry and anxiety (see Matthew 6:25-34 and Philippians 4:6-7). Take your prescription orally by reading these verses aloud twice a day, every day, until symptoms subside and you don't expect disaster in your future.

What about health? If you need healing find verses that promise God's provision of health, and then pray and declare them (see Exodus 15:26, 23:25, Matthew 8:16-17 and Acts 10:38). *"I will say of the Lord, 'He is my refuge and my fortress; my God, in Him I will trust'" (Psalm 91:2).* Say it loud! Say it often. Don't wait for sickness to attack your body, declare God's promises for a long healthy life now.

"With long life will He satisfy me and show me His salvation."
~Psalm 91:16

If you are experiencing financial lack, obey God in giving tithes and offerings (see Malachi 3:8-12), and then claim His great and precious promises of abundant provision (see 2 Corinthians 9:6-8 and Philippians 4:19). *"He is able to do exceedingly abundantly above all that we ask or think, according to the power that works in us" (Ephesians 3:20).* Listen to those three words, "exceedingly abundantly and above." This is the language of super sufficiency, of a supply that is over the top.

Declare the Word of God to any situation and watch it line up. I think we sometimes try to reap a harvest where there are no seeds sown. No seeds sown, no harvest. Lastly, we must have patience in sowing God's word. After you plant your seed, it takes time for that seed to mature until a harvest is achieved. There is a great harvest of faith ahead for those who esteem the powerful spiritual seed of God's Word. Your due season to reap God's blessings is on its way. Don't be impatient; persevere to the harvest. Faith and patience are the power twins of the Bible. Plant your seeds by faith and persevere to the harvest.

> *And let us not grow weary while doing good, for in due season we shall reap if we do not lose heart.* ~Galatians 6:9

> *Do not become sluggish but imitate those who through faith and patience inherit the promises.* ~Hebrews 6:12

> *Therefore be patient, brethren, until the coming of the Lord. See how the farmer waits for the precious fruit of the earth, waiting patiently for it until it receives the early and latter rain. You also be patient. Establish your hearts, for the coming of the Lord is at hand.* ~James 5:7-8

> *Therefore do not cast away your confidence, which has great reward. For you have need of endurance, so that after you have done the will of God, you may receive the promise.* ~Hebrews 10:35-36

THE HOLY SPIRIT TEACHES US THE BIBLE

> *Now we have received, not the spirit of the world, but the Spirit who is from God, that we might know the things that have been freely given to us by God. These things we also speak, not in words which man's wisdom teaches but which the Holy Spirit teaches, comparing spiritual things with spiritual. But the natural man does not receive the things of the Spirit of God, for they are foolishness to him; nor can he know them, because they are spiritually discerned.* ~1 Corinthians 2:12-14

God's Word is Spirit and Life

The mysteries of the Word of God are unsealed to the spiritual man, the person born again by the Spirit of God. The natural man cannot distinguish the hidden treasures of the book because they are spiritually discerned. The Holy Spirit is our teacher and wants to show us great and mighty things that we do not know (see Jeremiah 33:3). God is pouring out His Spirit in these last days and revealing mysteries to His faithful remnant church. He has promised to reveal secrets to His friends.

> **The secret of the LORD** *is with those who fear Him, and He will show them His covenant.* ~Psalm 25:14

> *For the perverse person is an abomination to the LORD, but* **His secret counsel** *is with the upright.* ~Proverbs 3:32

> *No longer do I call you servants, for a servant does not know what his master is doing; but I have called you friends, for all things that I heard from My Father* **I have made known to you**. ~John 15:15

> **He reveals deep and secret things**; *He knows what is in the darkness, and light dwells with Him.* ~Daniel 2:22

> *He answered and said to them,* **"Because it has been given to you to know the mysteries** *of the kingdom of heaven, but to them it has not been given."* ~Matthew 13:11

God is not stingy concerning His secrets. He wants to reveal things to you and me. If we will seek Him and make time to read the Holy Bible He will speak to us.

> *But the Helper, the Holy Spirit, whom the Father will send in My name, He will teach you all things, and bring to your remembrance all things that I said to you.* ~John 14:26

How can the Holy Spirit bring to your remembrance the things Jesus said if you don't know the things Jesus said? When you are reading your Bible, you are storing up a rich treasury of knowledge. The Holy Spirit will draw from that treasury and apply spiritual insight and wisdom to life's greatest challenges.

> *My son, keep your father's command, and do not forsake the law of your mother.*
> *Bind them continually upon your heart; tie them around your neck.*
> *When you roam, they will lead you; when you sleep, they will keep you;*
> *And when you awake, they will speak with you.*
> *For the commandment is a lamp, and the law a light; reproofs of instruction are the way of life.* ~Proverbs 6:20-23

READ YOUR BIBLE BY FAITH

For we walk by faith, not by sight. ~2 Corinthians 5:7

We walk by faith and not by sight. We also walk by faith and not by feelings. Feelings follow faith, not the other way around. If you are waiting for the right spiritual feelings to ignite your passion to read your Bible, or go to church, you will always be a nominal believer. A disciple cultivates spiritual discipline and positive life habits. A disciple doesn't get up in the morning and ask himself how he feels, he tells himself how to feel. An examined life is good, but too much introspection can be counterproductive. Sitting around asking yourself how you feel all the time can be an epic waste of time and a zap on your emotional strength.

We must learn to cultivate good life habits. The habits of life can be stronger than life itself, which is why it is so hard to change. Our habits and routines form our lifestyle. They say (whoever "they" are) that if you repeat something in your daily routine for 30 days it will become a new habit. There is a rhythm and groove to life habits. You can shove the gears of your brain into neutral and your body will just automatically go there. Or, you can motivate yourself into action. GET OFF THE COUCH!

For instance: If you pick a time in the day to read your Bible and spend time alone with God, and do it fairly consistently for a month, your spirit and mind will automatically be open and prepared to receive revelation from God and His word. When you get up in the morning, get your coffee and then open your Bible to a reading plan. Don't turn on the TV, and don't check your seven new emails or 12 notifications on Facebook. Go immediately to your Bible and ask God to show you great and mighty things that you know not (see Jeremiah 33:3). Your emails can wait. Checking how many likes you received from your latest posted selfie can wait. The positive affirmations from God will be so much better.

People sometimes tell me that they don't get anything from reading their Bible. Some tell me that they don't understand very much of what they are reading. I was asked to conduct a Bible study and minister to the young men in a Juvenile detention center, which was like a high security prison. These were the bad boys; rapists, drug dealers, some were convicted of armed robbery and some of murder. Many of these young men were to be transferred to prisons once they became of age. They were a hard lot. The Muslims in the prison were constantly harassing my students. They were trying to intimidate them and discourage them from coming to my Bible study. Some men attended because they were sending a message to those trying to intimidate them that they would not be bullied. (You're not the boss of me.)

SPIRIT WORLD

I asked my students to start reading their Bibles. I gave them a Bible through the year reading plan and told them that every week when we met I would ask them what they had read and then we would discuss it. After the first week I asked one of the guys what he had read. He said, "I didn't get anything out of my Bible reading. I think it was a waste of time."

I responded by asking, "What did you read?"

His answer was, "Well, I read the first three chapters of Genesis."

"So, tell me about it."

"I read that God created the world in six days and on the seventh day He rested. I thought to myself, 'That must be the reason we have seven days in a week.' I read that God spoke everything into existence and He made one man and one woman to populate the earth."

I was astonished and looked at the young man and said, "I thought you said you didn't get anything out of the Bible reading. It sounds like you got a lot out of it!"

He responded, "Oh yeah, I guess I did."

My point is that our feelings can deceive us. I guarantee that if you regularly read your Bible, you will receive tons from it. The Holy Spirit will begin to speak to you through the pages of God's Holy Book. You cannot feed on life and grace and not be filled with life and grace. You will be transformed by the renewing of your mind. You will be changed from glory to glory.

> *"I have not departed from the commandment of His lips; I have treasured the words of His mouth more than my necessary food."* ~Job 23:12

Chapter 5

INTRODUCTION TO DREAMS AND VISIONS

*And it shall come to pass in the last days, says God,
That I will pour out of My Spirit on all flesh;
Your sons and your daughters shall prophesy,
Your young men shall see visions,
Your old men shall dream dreams.* ~Acts 2:17

One of God's primary ways of communication is with visual pictures. Have you ever heard the old platitude "A picture is worth a thousand words"? It is so true. An image can speak volumes. You can receive insight from a visual image for years. Think of the dream that Joseph had of eleven sheaves of grain bowing down to his sheaf (see Genesis 37:5-8). This was a prophetic image of the future. Joseph's sheaf was a symbol of a fruitful life that would rise above his siblings. He would someday be so exalted that their sheaves would bow down to him. Although the images were symbolic, the dream was literally fulfilled. Joseph's brothers did bow down to him with their faces to the ground (see Genesis 42:6).

SPIRIT WORLD

Another interesting aspect of the dream is that Joseph's brothers were also represented by full sheaves of grain. Although Joseph's sheaf would rise above theirs, they would still be very fruitful and prosperous. This is what I'm saying; Joseph's one dream image contained a terabyte of information and it was easy to recall.

I believe we are living in the last days. As a deluge of God's Spirit is poured out on the earth, people from all tribes, nations and tongues will receive messages from God. Much of those messages will come in the form of dreams and visions. We need to know how to discern whether a dream or vision is from God. We need wisdom and insight in how to interpret these images, as not all dreams are messages from God. Our minds are amazing things, and there is a lot of information and emotions our minds have to process. Sometimes we are just working stuff out. Sometimes a dream is a reflection of a fear or challenge we are facing in life. Sometimes a dream is outright demonic and we need to reject everything about it.

I think it's amazing how God can get a message to us when our conscience mind is resting. He can bypass our grid of unbelief and logical scrutiny. He can speak directly to our spirit and subconscious mind. I think it's interesting that in the first two chapters of the book of Matthew, God speaks in dream form five times; four times to Joseph and once to the wise men (see Matthew 1:20, 2:12, 13, 19, 22). Every time, God gave them warning and direction. It's fascinating that the Joseph of the New Testament was a dreamer like the Joseph of the book of Genesis.

God sometimes used dreams to communicate His will in the book of Acts. One particular story is found in Acts 16:6-10: Paul's missionary team was forbidden by the Holy Spirit to go into Asia and Bithynia. This was a timing thing with God. There would be a time to go into these regions but this wasn't it. Then the Apostle Paul had a vision of the night (this is another way of saying that he had a dream). In the dream there was a man from Macedonia that pleaded with them to come over and help them. Paul conveyed the night vision to his team and they came to a conclusion that it was from God. This was how it was done in the book of Acts. They didn't do a demographics study and a saturation study of the region to see if it would support a church. God told them in a dream to go; they prayed about it, the whole group received a witness from the Holy Spirit, and they went.

I knew a young minister who felt as though God wanted him to take a failed church and revitalize it. He was on staff at a large stable church at the time, and he and his family had security in that church. As he contemplated the move to the smaller community to be the senior pastor of the failed church, he began to over think things. He did the demographic studies. He canvassed the neighborhoods. He would go on and on about the viability of being successful at this church. I finally had enough of his overanalyzing and I said to him, "Here is the bottom line, does God want you to pastor this church or not? I think that you're more than ready to take it on and be successful, but you have to hear from God for yourself. You're not going to take all the risk out of faith, otherwise it's not faith."

Apparently the speech had an effect. A month later I met up with him and his wife. His wife thanked me for slapping him up with my little speech, as none of her wifely encouragement was having an effect. He decided to go for it and the church is a thriving church today. The moral of the story is that God wants to talk to us and lead us today. Demographic studies are good, but in the end you have to hear from God and take a faith risk. One of the ways that God confirms to us His will is through dreams and visions. All visions must line up with the inner witness of the Holy Spirit and the Word of God.

> *Then He said, "Hear now My words:*
> *If there is a prophet among you,*
> *I, the LORD, make Myself known to him in a vision;*
> *I speak to him in a dream."* ~Numbers 12:6

When the Holy Spirit was poured out in Acts chapter 2, prophetic gifting was imparted to the church. Are you a member of THE church universal? If you are a believer and Jesus is your Lord and Savior, then the spirit of the prophets is upon you. I would venture to say that every Christian has had a dream from God at one time or another.

Do you remember in chapter three of this book, "The Still Small Voice", where I shared with you about the different levels of hearing from God? The higher the level of revelation, the rarer the occurrence. As far as the voice of God is concerned there are three levels:

1. The inner witness, impression, conscience, intuition, or knowing
2. The inner audible voice
3. The audible voice of God

Hearing an audible voice from God would be the highest form of revelation (other than the written Word of God, of course) and would occur most infrequently. Dreams and visions have levels as well. The first level is the most common, while the last and highest levels are uncommon and occur the most infrequently.

1. **Dreams**, or visions of the night, are like the inner witness that every Christian has experienced.
2. **Closed Vision**: This is a vision in your mind. When I say "cow" you visualize a cow in your mind. A closed vision could be a snapshot picture, or a short movie in your mind's eye.

Introduction to Dreams and Visions

3. **Open Vision**: This is a visual picture, or short movie outside of you and in front of you. You are still aware of your surroundings but can clearly recognize that you are seeing a vision from God.

4. **Trances**: This is where you are awake but caught up into the vision, so much so that you are unaware of your surroundings. Paul said, *"Whether in the body I do not know, or whether out of the body I do not know" (2 Corinthians 12:2)*. Paul was caught up into the third heaven. Peter experienced a trance as described in Acts 10:9-13. In Revelation 4:1, the Apostle John was translated into the future and into heaven. His vision was interactive; he recorded and wrote while he was there! He interacted with angels who handed him scrolls and gave explanation to what he was seeing and experiencing!

I'm entering a disclaimer before we go further. All the dreams, visions and trances in the Bible were not brought on by any self-achieved altered state of consciousness. They didn't chant or use breathing techniques to achieve some REM state of consciousness to self-induce a vision. They didn't initiate the visions by visualization techniques such as imagining Jesus sitting with them at a beach. They didn't use drugs like peyote, marijuana or any other mind-altering hallucinogen. These practices are types of sorcery and can bring demonic oppression and false visions. God does not want you to ever be in a vulnerable position where your judgment is impaired, or where your defenses are down and you are open to demonic influence. The Bible encourages a sober mind (see Titus 2:2 and 1 Peter 1:13, 5:8). All forms of sorcery are forbidden (see Deuteronomy 18:10-12 and Galatians 5:20).

> *And they did not repent of their murders or their sorceries or their sexual immorality or their thefts.* ~Revelation 9:21

SPIRIT WORLD

The word for sorcery in the New Testament is the Greek word pharmakeia (Strong's #5331) from which we get our English words pharmacy, and pharmacist. This word is generally used for drugs, medicine, or spells. Sorcery is illicit drug use accompanied by incantations, charms and magic. If you are using hallucinogenic drugs you are inadvertently subjecting yourself to demonic influence.

> *So Saul died for his unfaithfulness which he had committed against the LORD, because he did not keep the word of the LORD, and also because he consulted a medium for guidance. But he did not inquire of the LORD; therefore He killed him, and turned the kingdom over to David the son of Jesse.*
> ~1 Chronicles 10:13-14

King Saul came under the judgment of God because he sought spiritual experience outside of God's safe zone. How would you like your epitaph to be like his? Seeking mediums, psychics and fortune tellers, or seeking visions by drug use are not good ideas.

If God wants you to have a supernatural experience He will bring it to you. *"But seek first the kingdom of God and His righteousness, and all these things shall be added to you" (Matthew 6:33).* All you have to worry about is going after God, everything you need will be added to your journey. If you strive to have certain experiences, you may start making things up. The dreams and visions that I personally experienced were never self-induced. It was pretty obvious that these experiences were from God. I never had to chant mantras or provoke these experiences with visualization techniques or drugs. Having spiritual experiences is NOT what makes you a spiritual person, or a spiritually mature Christian. Having a refined and proven character by walking out your salvation with fear and trembling; being mighty in the scriptures and applying them to your life; laying a good foundation for this life and the life to come; THESE are the things that make you spiritual. We can pray for experiences, but let God be sovereign. When we read about the qualifications for elders and deacons in the local church, not once does the Bible say that they must have a third heaven experience or hear an audible voice to qualify as a spiritual leader. It's all about having a proven character (see 1 Timothy 3:1-12).

I will say this though, you can position yourself to receive more visions and hear from God. Most of the spiritual experiences that I've had were in church during extended prayer meetings, powerful worship services, and at the altar during prayer times. Don't avoid God encounters. Are you afraid that God will tell you to do something that you don't want to do? Are you afraid that He will chastise you in some way? Don't be afraid and don't avoid spirit-filled church services. God is crazy about you. He loves you and wants the best for you. When God-hungry, humble, and holy people get together, God shows up in powerful ways. Get your butt in church! (My editor suggested other synonyms: bum, buns, bottom, backside, keester, lower self, derriere, tooshie, booty.)

> *For where two or three are gathered together in My name, I am there in the midst of them.* ~Matthew 18:20

> *And let us consider one another in order to stir up love and good works, not forsaking the assembling of ourselves together, as is the manner of some, but exhorting one another, and so much the more as you see the Day approaching.*
> ~Hebrews 10:24-25

In the next chapter I share with you some dreams and visions that I've had. These experiences were very significant to me and were life altering.

If God wants you to have a supernatural experience He will bring it to you.

Chapter 6

THE DREAM WEAVER

For God may speak in one way, or in another,
Yet man does not perceive it.
In a dream, in a vision of the night,
When deep sleep falls upon men,
While slumbering on their beds,
Then He opens the ears of men,
And seals their instruction.
In order to turn man from his deed,
And conceal pride from man,
He keeps back his soul from the Pit,
And his life from perishing by the sword. ~Job 33:14-18

Never underestimate the love of God. The extent that God will go to reach out to sinners is mind blowing. In the above scripture God uses dreams to communicate to man. His intent is to turn man from his own purpose and to keep him from perishing. I have heard stories of Jesus coming to unsaved people in dreams. I believe them. I was one of those people that God came to in dreams. God, in His love, was reaching out to me. Could it be that someone was praying for me? Because of the dreams that I had received from God, and how they helped lead me to Christ, I have no problem praying that God would give dreams to my unsaved friends and family. In the solemnity of night when deep sleep falls on man, the Dream Weaver is at work sowing together a beautiful tapestry of revelation.

THE DREAM OF THE GREAT WHITE THRONE JUDGMENT

A few years before I gave my life to Christ I had a dream. This dream changed my life and was a key component in leading me to a saving knowledge of Christ. In the dream I was standing before Jesus who was sitting on a great white throne. I can't give you any details about the throne except that it was big and white. Jesus was in white Middle Eastern clothing. He had wavy, shoulder length hair with piercing brown eyes. As I looked up to the elevated throne, the look on His face was of a calm confidence. He had a look in His eyes that communicated He knew something I didn't, and He was confident of the outcome.

There was an angel on His right side, and an angel on His left. The angel on His right side was big and muscular. He had on a long white robe as well. All of his features were dark. He had shoulder length thick dark hair and coal black eyes. When I looked into his eyes I immediately wanted to look away. He was scary. His huge hands rested on the hilt of a massive sword in front of him. I just knew he was protector and enforcer. He was the executioner. He was the consummate warrior. I did not want to mess with the guy on the throne with that angel standing there. The angel watched everything I did as I stood before Him to whom I must give account. He was the personification of judgment.

The angel on the left side of Jesus was the opposite in many ways. He had lighter features; shoulder length, wavy dishwater blond hair and piercing blue eyes. When I looked into his eyes I immediately felt empathy and compassion. I believe he was the representative of mercy. In front of the mercy angel was an ornate, huge wooden podium. There was a holder in the center where large scrolls were stored for easy access. A very large scroll was open on the lectern and the mercy angel was searching for something as he ran his finger up and down the page. He would search and then look up at me with concern and empathy.

Although no words were spoken, volumes were communicated to me in this night vision. When the angel of mercy had trouble finding my name in the grand scroll, a dreadful feeling swept over me. I started to feel panic rise up within me, and then I woke up in that dread state. I knew that my eternal future was being deliberated. For the first time I pondered whether I would go to heaven or be turned to hell. I never had to ask the question, "Was this dream from God or not?" I knew it was from God.

Another thing you have to understand is that I knew there was a judgment day in the future, but I didn't know anything about a Great White Throne Judgment or anything about a Book of Life. You can imagine how flabbergasted I was when I discovered that there was a Book of Life and a Great White Throne Judgment!

> Then **I saw a great white throne and Him who sat on it,** from whose face the earth and the heaven fled away. And there was found no place for them. And I saw the dead, small and great, standing before God, **and books were opened. And another book was opened, which is the Book of Life.** And the dead were judged according to their works, by the things which were written in the books. The sea gave up the dead who were in it, and Death and Hades delivered up the dead who were in

> them. And they were judged, each one according to his works. Then Death and Hades were cast into the lake of fire. This is the second death. **And anyone not found written in the Book of Life was cast into the lake of fire.** ~Revelation 20:11-15

The Bible tells us that books will be opened at the final judgment. What books? We know for sure that there is a Book of Life that contains the names of all the redeemed. Think of it, every person found worthy of eternal life from the creation of mankind will have their name written in that amazing book.

> And I urge you also, true companion, help these women who labored with me in the gospel, with Clement also, and the rest of my fellow workers, whose names are in the **Book of Life**.
> ~Philippians 4:3

> He who overcomes shall be clothed in white garments, and I will not blot out his name from the **Book of Life**; but I will confess his name before My Father and before His angels.
> ~Revelation 3:5

> All who dwell on the earth will worship Him, whose names have not been written in the **Book of Life** of the Lamb slain from the foundation of the world. ~Revelation 13:8

There are a few other references to the Book of Life and its importance. Can you imagine the responsibility of being the keeper and recorder of such a book? I am so glad the angel in charge of the Book of Life had a disposition of great mercy.

Other books that will be opened and referenced at the Great White Throne Judgment include the books of the Bible. Jesus said that we will be judged by the words He has spoken. This would account for the many books I saw in my dream that were neatly packed in the large ornate podium the angel was standing behind.

He who rejects Me, and does not receive My words, has that which judges him — the word that I have spoken will judge him in the last day. ~John 12:48

There are several heavenly record books mentioned in the Bible. There are probably volumes that we do not know about. In the Gospel of John, he states that he could not possibly have written everything that Jesus did. *"I suppose that even the world itself could not contain the books that would be written" (John 21:25)*. Here are a few other heavenly record books mentioned in the Bible:

- **The book of the Wars of the Lord** (see Numbers 21:14): While this may be a reference to a lost book that did not make it into the Jewish cannon (measured as authentic) of scripture, it still seems feasible that a record would be kept of all holy wars, both on earth and in the heaven lies among the angels.

- **The Book of Tears:** *"You number my wanderings; put my tears into Your bottle; are they not in Your book" (Psalm 56:8)?* It's beyond the scope of our imagination that God is so caring and concerned about you and me that He keeps a record of every tear we shed and every heartache we experience.

- **The Book of Details:** In Psalm 139:15-16, there is mention of records made of every detail of the psalmist's body. God is so intimate with us and our lives that Jesus said that every hair on our head is numbered (see Luke 12:7). Amazing! Every detail of our lives is recorded. Jesus said that we would give account of every idle word that we speak (see Matthew 12:36). There is probably a whole bookshelf dedicated to my atrocious idle words. How much writer's cramp have I alone caused the angels? The world may never know.

- There is a **Book of Remembrance** for those who fear the Lord and speak of Him (see Malachi 3:16). God is mindful of His faithful servants. While the world slanders and scandalizes faith in Christ, there will always be those who resolve to trust God and continue to speak well of Him. *"Blessed are those who have not seen and yet have believed" (John 20:29b).* The highest form of faith is believing when you don't understand (see Proverbs 3:5-6).

Another interesting aspect to the dream was the imposing angel with the sword. I have wondered through the years if this was the same angel that is mentioned in the Bible who brought a plague on Israel after King David ordered the numbering of the nation. David saw him standing between earth and heaven with his sword drawn and stretched out over Jerusalem (see 1 Chronicles 21:14-16). Could this have been the same angel of judgment that I saw in my dream? I wonder if it's the same angel that single-handedly wiped out 185 thousand Assyrian soldiers who were poised and ready to attack Jerusalem (see Isaiah 37:36).

When I think of the two angels standing at the right and left side of Christ, I think of the balance between mercy and judgment; the goodness and severity of God.

> *Therefore consider the goodness and severity of God: on those who fell, severity; but toward you, goodness, if you continue in His goodness. Otherwise you also will be cut off.*
> *~Romans 11:22*

We are admonished to consider both the goodness and severity of God. There seems to always be extreme imbalances one way or the other. One camp of believers will focus only on the severity of God. Their main method of evangelism is to scare the daylights out of you by presenting God as an angry seething giant about to descend upon your life, wielding thunder bolts of vengeance because all your evil deeds deserve a reckoning.

Another camp glosses over all negative images of the judgment side of God. They are like toxic drug pushers of false extreme grace. When an addicted user and abuser of false grace has to deal with the reality that God sometimes says NO, when they realize that He is NOT always affirming everything they want to do, when they realize that God sometimes chastises and admonishes those He loves, then they experience withdrawals and delirium tremors. They may go into extreme confusion when they are smitten with the reality that their faith was built on the illusion that God was their personal genie. The truth that eternal hell awaits the unrepentant sinner is too much to handle. It's much easier to believe that all will be saved in the end, even Adolf Hitler, Joseph Stalin and Jack the Ripper.

Dishonest scales are an abomination to the LORD,
But a just weight is His delight. ~Proverbs 11:1

So speak and so do as those who will be judged by the law
of liberty. For judgment is without mercy to the one who has
shown no mercy. Mercy triumphs over judgment.
~James 2:12-13

I am so glad that mercy triumphs over judgment. The judgment side of God demanded retribution for the sins of mankind. The mercy side of God provided a sacrifice in Christ. Those who accept that sacrifice escape the retribution of God. *"Choose life that both you and your descendants may live" (Deuteronomy 30:19b).*

The dream I had of standing before the Great White Throne Judgment still speaks. Those images are burned into my conscious and subconscious mind. *"When deep sleep falls upon men, while slumbering* on their beds. *Then He opens the ears of men and seals their instruction. In order to turn man from his deed and conceal pride from man. He keeps his soul from the Pit, and his life from perishing by the sword" (Job 33:15b-18).* God still speaks to us in dreams today. You will know if a dream is from God. You won't have to guess. May God give you an interpretation that leads to peace.

THE DREAM OF THE RESTAURANT AND GIVING MY PORTION TO CHRIST

When I was in High School, I had a class where I sat beside a German exchange student. I really liked this guy and found him very interesting to talk to. I came to school troubled by a dream I had the night before. My changed countenance did not go unnoticed by my German friend. I told him I had a weird dream and asked if he knew anything about dream interpretation. He explained that he had studied dream symbolism in psychology classes and that he would like to at least hear the dream and analyze the various components. I thought to myself, "This will be a fun game. I wonder what Sigmund Freud has to say about my dreams."

In the dream I was sitting at a large table in the back of an upscale restaurant. This was some sort of meeting place for the rich and powerful. Everyone at the table was dressed in expensive tuxedo style clothing. Some of us even had black top hats. Several waiters hovered around our table and delivered heaping plates of fine dining cuisine. As the panoramic scene moved outward from my table, I could see that the front of the restaurant had an open-air café. There was a black, ornate, cast iron fence around the perimeter of the outdoor patio. Many people from the street crowded up to the fence reaching through the bars with outstretched hands to beg for food. The clothing style of those people resembled that of a third world Middle Eastern country. The fancy dressed maître d'hôtel would occasionally approach the fence and chase the beggars away but to no avail; they would eventually gather and beg again. One man somehow breached security and was sitting at a table. I knew that the maître d'hôtel would soon spot the underdressed man and a scene would erupt when the man was asked to leave. I arose from my table, with my plate of food, and sat down next to the poor beggar. The head waiter approached the table and was about to ask the man to leave when I stopped him and said that he was with me. At that, the head waiter's eye brows went up, and then he turned on his heels and walked off. When I looked at the beggar more closely, I realized that it was Jesus, the Christ. I then slid my entire plate over to him and he looked at me with a self-confident, approving look.

Immediately after telling my dream to the German exchange student, he began his straight forward simplistic interpretation. "You will leave a life of privilege and give your portion to Christ. The plate of food symbolizes your whole life. You will someday give your life to the service of Christ."

I was completely floored by his interpretation. Instead of some Freudian archetypes, the guy foretells my future like some gypsy. This was a prophetic word that eventually was fulfilled. The divine irony about this whole scenario was that neither one of us were "born again" Christians. Far from it. Our lifestyles were that of total heathens. The fact that God would give a dream to an unbeliever, and then have it interpreted prophetically by another unbeliever, made this kind of miraculous.

There was a situation in the Bible where Gideon was called by God to lead the Israelites to victory against their oppressors. Gideon was frightened and the Spirit of God told him to sneak up close to the enemy encampment at night, and then listen to what they were saying around the camp fire. After hearing their conversation, his hands were strengthened for the upcoming battle (see Judges 7:9-15).

> *And when Gideon had come, there was a man telling a dream to his companion. He said, "I have had a dream: To my surprise, a loaf of barley bread tumbled into the camp of Midian; it came to a tent and struck it so that it fell and overturned, and the tent collapsed."*
> *Then his companion answered and said, "This is nothing else but the sword of Gideon the son of Joash, a man of Israel! Into his hand God has delivered Midian and the whole camp."*
> ~Judges 7:13-14

What made this extra miraculous was that God gave a dream to an unbeliever and it was interpreted prophetically by another unbeliever. Oh the extent that God will go to get your attention and give you an encouraging word. What a great God we serve.

THE DREAM OF THE DISTRACTED CHURCH

I want to start out by saying that I love my church. I love the people that the Lord has privileged me to pastor. I take the charge to shepherd God's flock very seriously. Sometimes I feel overwhelmed with the responsibility to preach and teach the Word of God. I want to please the Lord with the right word at the right time that will bless, and not curse. I always want to make sure the people of God are encouraged, with their faith built up. If I have to bring a strong challenge to the church, I pray about it and check my motivations. I want to minister a pure word from a pure heart. That being said, there are times the Lord impresses on me to bring a strong admonishment to the church. It's definitely not my favorite thing to do.

The Dream Weaver

One Saturday night as I went to bed, I was confident with my message for Sunday morning service. It was a good encouraging word. I always want to be open to any changes the Lord wants to make in the message, but I have a hard time if the Spirit impresses on me to preach something edgy, or harsh. It's not my thing. I usually try to get out of it. But when He persists, I believe I obey most of the time.

During that Saturday night I dreamt I was preaching a good profound word to the church. As I kept rolling on with boat loads of Holy Ghost revelation, folks started to have conversations with one another. It was subtle at first, but then they became more overt and loud. I could actually hear some of the conversations. They were joking and laughing like they were at a restaurant and I was just background noise. It wasn't just a few people; it was almost everyone, even those who I would consider the more pious of the bunch. They were talking about what they were going do after the service; how their children were doing; their favorite programs on TV; where they were going on vacation this year. It was very inappropriate behavior in church while I was speaking. I started to get angry. At first I was angry for myself because I felt personally disrespected. Then I realized that the people were disrespecting God by their rude behavior. I was angry and formulating how I was going to rebuke the people when I woke up. I woke up angry.

While I was considering the dream, God spoke to me in an inner audible voice, "Tell my people that they are distracted by many things and they are not listening to me. The way that you feel right now is a little of what I feel." Wow, this will be interesting. Change of plans. I had such a nice sermon all planned too, oh well.

I put together some notes before the service about distractions. I'm almost sure they contained the story of Mary and Martha (see Luke 10:38-42); Mary sat at Jesus' feet to hear the Word, while Martha was distracted with serving. However, nothing turned out like I had planned. I simply got up and reiterated the dream that I had the night before. I shared how angry I was; first for myself and then at the disrespect for God. Then I shared what God said after I woke up, "Tell my people that they are distracted by many things and they are not listening to me. The way you feel right now is a little of what I feel."

After I shared the dream and what God had said, I opened the altar for folks to respond to what God showed me in the dream. What happened next was amazing. The whole church, as though one person, got up and came rushing forward. For the next 45 minutes folks wept, prayed and asked God for forgiveness. We had a wonderful altar ministry time praying for one another.

As preachers of righteousness, we have to share the message that God gives us. We can't hem and haw, or be intimidated by people's facial expressions. We must love God, and love His flock enough to be obedient.

> *"I have not sent these prophets, yet they ran.*
> *I have not spoken to them, yet they prophesied.*
> *But if they had stood in My counsel,*
> *And had caused My people to hear My words,*
> *Then they would have turned them from their evil way*
> *And from the evil of their doings.   ~Jeremiah 23:21-22*

Things have not changed much since the days of Jeremiah. Technology has advanced, and people are generally more educated, but man himself has not changed. If anything, man has become a more clever devil. We still have the same flawed nature that men had in the days of Jeremiah. Preachers still fail to wait on God for the right message to be delivered.

The hardest part of my job as a preacher of righteousness is waiting on God for the right subject matter. I can put sermon notes together on any subject. It's a gift. God has anointed me by the Holy Spirit to teach the Bible. The real challenge is knowing the right word of encouragement God has for His people.

> *The Lord GOD has given Me*
> *The tongue of the learned,*
> *That I should know how to speak*
> *A word in season to him who is weary.*
> *He awakens Me morning by morning,*
> *He awakens My ear*
> *To hear as the learned.* ~Isaiah 50:4
>
> *A man has joy by the answer of his mouth,*
> *And a word spoken in due season, how good it is!*
> ~Proverbs 15:23

My prayer is that God would give you the right word, at the right time; a word spoken in due season. May the Dream Weaver create beautiful tapestries, heavenly messages in profound colors.

> *Then He opens the ears of men and seals their instruction.*
> ~Job 33:16

*Visions and visual pictures are a large part
of the language of the Spirit*

Chapter 7

VISIONS

I will stand my watch
And set myself on the rampart,
And watch to see what He will say to me,
And what I will answer when I am corrected. ~Habakkuk 2:1

The Prophet said that he would watch to see what God would say. Visions and visual pictures are a large part of the language of the Spirit. Hearing from God is the heritage of every believer (see John 10:27-28, Acts 2:17-18 and Revelation 3:20). A vast amount of that communication will be in visual pictures. A relationship with God is a two-way street. He wants to talk to you, as much or more, than you want to talk to Him. Our relationship with God wasn't meant to be a one-sided monologue from us to Him; it was meant to be a dialogue. A one-sided relationship never works.

We can be like the prophet Habakkuk and position ourselves to hear from God. He positioned himself on a watch; a time of prayer, reflection

SPIRIT WORLD

and Bible reading. I call this a private devotional time. To hear from God more, we must set aside time to meet with Him.

- **Meet with God** by having a regular devotional time.

- **Watch and look** for visions, or visual pictures. Once, while reading my Bible, a friend came to mind, and while I was thinking of him a scripture verse came to my mind. I immediately texted the Bible verse to him, and within a minute he texted me back: *"You don't know how much you just made me a believer, I believe!! I just had an awful phone call and you sent this. I'm almost in tears."*

- **Listen** to what He will say to you through the Word of God, inner witness, or in a still small voice.

    Then the LORD answered me and said:
    "Write the vision
    And make it plain on tablets,
    That he may run who reads it.
    For the vision is yet for an appointed time;
    But at the end it will speak, and it will not lie.
    Though it tarries, wait for it;
    Because it will surely come,
    It will not tarry." ~Habakkuk 2:2-3

- **Write the vision.** Get in the habit of keeping a journal of what the Spirit is teaching and showing you. Keeping a dream journal is also good. When you suspect a dream or vision may be from God, write it down and pray for understanding.

- **Wait for it.** Wait on the Lord to give understanding. Wait on Him to bring things to pass.

    It is doubtless not profitable for me to boast. I will come to visions and revelations of the Lord. ~2 Corinthians 12:1

Notice the confession of the Apostle Paul, *"I will come to visions and revelations of the Lord."* This should be our confession as well. We are living in a time when the Holy Spirit is being poured out on all flesh. Visions and dreams are becoming more common place (see Acts 2:17). Spiritual experiences should not cause us to be boastful. If you start thinking you're on a higher spiritual plane than everyone else, you're in trouble. "God resists the proud, but gives grace to the humble. Therefore humble yourselves under the mighty hand of God, that He may exalt you in due time" (1 Peter 5:5b-6).

Not every vision and dream is from God. But by being a student of the Bible and staying submitted to wise, mature, spiritual leadership, you will develop the proper discernment to evaluate visions and dreams.

> *Beloved, do not believe every spirit, but test the spirits, whether they are of God; because many false prophets have gone out into the world.* ~1 John 4:1

> *Do not quench the Spirit. Do not despise prophecies.* **Test all things**; *hold fast what is good.* ~1 Thessalonians 5:19-21

The ultimate test is to measure experience by the Word of God. Are there similar experiences in the Bible? What is the fruit of the experience? Does it bring glory to God? Or, does it bring glory to a person? Does it coincide with the character of God, as revealed in scripture?

Lastly, we must keep in mind that spiritual experience is not the goal. Knowing God is the goal. Drawing closer to Him, seeking Him first, and knowing His will for our life. "Seek first the Kingdom of God, and His righteousness, and all these things will be added to you" (Matthew 6:33). When God is first place, everything stays in its proper order. Spiritual experiences just happen when we seek God. If we seek spiritual experiences first we risk being like Simon the Sorcerer. He sought to buy the power of God with money. Not because he wanted to glorify God but because he wanted to bring glory to himself and use the power of God to enrich himself and have control over others. Prophetic gifting and the powers of the world to come are for the humble, the hungry, and the holy. They are for our service to one another. They are not for the haughty; boasters beware. The rebuke of Peter stands true today for self-glorifying power seekers today.

But Peter said to him (Simon the Sorcerer), *"Your money perish with you, because you thought that the gift of God could be purchased with money! You have neither part nor portion in this matter, for your heart is not right in the sight of God. Repent therefore of this your wickedness, and pray God if perhaps the thought of your heart may be forgiven you. For I see that you are poisoned by bitterness and bound by iniquity." (Acts 8:20-23).*

THE VISION OF THE RAGGED CHILDREN

It was New Year's Eve and we were making our way on a highway along the icy coast of Lake Michigan. We had heard about a remote campground where an all-night prayer meeting was being held. Believers from all over west Michigan were gathering there to pray in the New Year. I was pastoring a church in northern lower Michigan at the time, and had brought some friends from the church to experience a good all-night prayer meeting.

The worship bands were amazing and the presence of God was very thick in the meeting room. Interspersed with the anointed worship, prophetic words were given. There was even some spontaneous preaching and sharing from the Word of God. This is where I wanted to be on this New Year's Eve, with a Spirit-filled, Charismatic group that was willing to just let the Holy Spirit flow.

As the night marched on, it felt as though the atmosphere became more and more charged with the Holy Spirit's presence. I was on my knees totally engaged in worship. I opened my eyes and I thought I saw a child dressed in ragged clothes on his hands and knees picking crumbs up off the floor. I put my hand on the shoulder of my friend next to me and asked if he had seen a child crawling around the floor. He gave me a funny look and said that he hadn't. It was then that I realized God was trying to speak to me, so I asked Him to show me the vision again. Right in front of me there was a boy and a girl this time. They looked to be between 7 and 10 years of age. They were dressed in rags and were picking up crumbs off the floor and quickly putting the meager morsels in their mouths. If they were real children that someone had brought to the meeting I would have immediately called child protective services. After a few minutes the vision was gone.

This was an open vision. It wasn't in my mind's eye it was outside of me, in front of me. I wasn't in a trance, I was still aware of my surroundings but captivated by the visual display in front of me.

This vision left me upset. The state of the children in the vision made me angry and I asked God what this vision could mean? This is what I felt He was telling me: *"This is what the children in My church look like. They're feeding off the crumbs that fall from the table of the adults."*

I realized that the crumbs the children were feeding on were spiritual crumbs. They were getting even less than the leftovers. Children were not getting ministered to properly. Most of our money, and the best teachers, were focused on adult ministries. Our children were getting the scraps. There needed to be a greater focus given on the next generation. *"One generation shall praise Your works to another, and shall declare Your mighty acts" (Psalm 145:4).* Consequently, we determined to make children's ministry a greater priority in our church. Not just children, but

SPIRIT WORLD

teenagers, college-age adults and young married couples. The alternative is a generation that doesn't know the Lord.

> *⁷ So the people served the LORD all the days of Joshua, and all the days of the elders who outlived Joshua, who had seen all the great works of the LORD which He had done for Israel.*
>
> *¹⁰ When all that generation had been gathered to their fathers,* ***another generation arose after them who did not know the LORD*** *nor the work which He had done for Israel.*
>
> *¹¹ Then the children of Israel did evil in the sight of the LORD, and served the Baals.* ~Judges 2:7, 10-11

How could this happen? The generation following the Joshua generation did not KNOW God! The Joshua generation had known great victories. They saw the sun stand still until they had victory over their enemies. They experienced God's help in defeating giants and armies with chariots of iron. Somehow the Joshua generation failed to pass on this legacy.

The question that begs to be asked is, "What does it mean to know God?" The Hebrew word for "know" is "yada" (Strong's #3045), it means to know by experience, and in some cases in the Bible it means to know intimately (see Genesis 4:1, 25). It's not enough for our children to know ABOUT God, they need to experience Him. They need a personal God encounter. The Prophet Samuel had this kind of personal encounter with God when he was just a child.

> *Then the LORD called yet again, "Samuel!" So Samuel arose and went to Eli, and said, "Here I am, for you called me." He answered, "I did not call, my son; lie down again." (Now Samuel did not yet know the LORD, nor was the word of the LORD yet revealed to him.)* ~1 Samuel 3:6-7

The Priest Eli was sensitive enough to know that God was revealing Himself to the boy and he mentored Samuel. Samuel was being trained as a priest, in all the knowledge of God, but that wasn't enough. This personal encounter with God began Samuel on a trajectory to be a great leader and prophet to the nation of Israel. Oh, how our children need divine encounters with God at the altars of children's church, church camp, and special services. Food, fun and friends are all good and well, but they also need opportunities to know Jesus personally.

THE VISION OF JESUS STANDING IN FRONT OF THE DRUM SET

Right around the time I had the dream about the Great White Throne Judgment (described in chapter 6) I also had an open vision of Jesus. I was a young man of about 20 years and not serving the Lord wholeheartedly at the time. I was home alone while watching the old classic film "The Greatest Story Ever Told" which is about the life of Christ. This film had the all-star cast of its day. There was a lot of the Bible referenced within the lines of the movie. The scene of Jesus preaching the Sermon on the Mount found in Matthew 5-7 really struck me. The sheer goodness of the words spoken made me think that this could only have come from a holy God, a mere man would never have thought of this. We are too evil, spiteful and vengeful in our nature to produce such eloquent, virtuous words. The goodness of the Sermon on the Mount is a great proof for the Bible being authored by the Holy Spirit and not man.

> *Knowing this first, that no prophecy of Scripture is of any private interpretation, for prophecy never came by the will of man, but holy men of God spoke as they were moved by the Holy Spirit.* ~2 Peter 1:20-21

SPIRIT WORLD

After the movie was over I went downstairs to practice playing my drum kit. I was taking lessons at the time and practicing an average of two to three hours a day. In a few months' time, I surpassed all of the other students at the music school (some of them had been taking lessons for a couple of years). I was quite focused on becoming a Rock Star. Before I began my practice session, I was leaning against the doorpost admiring the beauty and utter coolness of my drum kit. As I took another puff of my cigarette, Jesus appeared in front of me in a ghost-like image. (There wasn't any funny stuff in that smoke, I swear.) Two things happened immediately: I got goose bumps all over my body, and I put my cigarette out directly.

No words were spoken. He looked at me and then looked at my drum kit. He had a loving, confident look on his face like when I saw Him in my dream of the Great White Throne Judgment. His eyes looked right through me. I just knew that the thoughts and motives of my heart were easily exposed. There is no point in playing games with the Son of God.

Even though there were no words spoken, I knew what He was asking of me. He wanted me to surrender my life to Him and dedicate all my abilities and talents for His use. And then, in a flash, He was gone and the vision ended. I was a little dumbfounded for a few moments. Then I foolishly thought I could make a deal with Him. How absurd it is to try to make bargains with God almighty. I said to Him, "I'll tell you what, if you help me to become a famous Rock Star, then when I become a radical Christian it will have a greater impact." LOL (Current texting and social media jargon for "Laugh out loud". When I first saw "LOL" I had no idea what I was looking at.)

There are no deals with God. You are not going to be able to manipulate Him. Here's the real deal, you give Him your broken and messed up life and He puts the robe of righteousness on you; He gives you the ring of royal sonship and elevates you to be a co-heir with Jesus (see Romans 8:17). Nothing less than the total surrender of your life will suffice. Jesus is not really Lord of all unless you are willing to surrender all. The beauty of a life completely surrendered to Jesus never ceases to inspire and amaze. Our gifts put into the Master's hand will multiply and yield a cornucopia of fruit. God's plan is always best. He created you and he knows what will bring you fulfillment and joy.

About a year after I became born again, I surrendered all of my selfish ambitions. Jesus was able to use my music after I put it down for a season. If we fail to surrender our selfish ambitions to Jesus, we end up trying to impose those ambitions onto God, expecting Him to bless and fulfill them. Instead of having the ambition to become a secular Rock Star, you will transfer that desire into your new walk with Christ and want to become a Christian Rock Star. There is nothing wrong with wanting to do great things for God, but what if those ambitions aren't achieved? If God doesn't fulfill your ambition, and jump through your hoops the way you want, will you backslide? Will you walk away from Him because He didn't give you what you wanted, when you wanted it? I love what God told Abraham: *After these things the word of the LORD came to Abram in a vision, saying, "Do not be afraid, Abram. I am your shield, your exceedingly great reward." (Genesis 15:1).*

To have God Himself as an exceedingly great reward is all you will ever need. When you have Him, the entire universe is at your fingertips. All you need, want, hope for, or imagine, are in Him. When God becomes your all in all, everything else is just icing on the cake. Fulfilled desires and stuff are just extra little rewards next to the exceeding great reward of God Himself.

SPIRIT WORLD

THE VISION OF JESUS WITH THE HEAVY SACK

When I was going to Bible College and living on my own, I decided to go wife hunting. (Track with me before you think I was all carnal.) My line of reasoning at the time was that I needed a good Christian wife who wanted to marry a future minister. I was in my early 20's and wanted to get married THEN! I wondered: *"Where am I going to find a good woman?"* Certainly not in a night club, and the girls at my workplace were not serving the Lord. This predicament left a limited hunting ground for perspective talent. Church was obviously one option. Another was the colleges and universities in my area.

Central Michigan University was only 45 minutes from where I lived and I heard of a rocking Christian fellowship that met on the campus. Sign me up. It was a fantastic charismatic fellowship group; there must have been 100 students that attended the services. I made friends quickly and had a few "fish on the hook" until God told me not to date any of the girls there. I didn't realize that I wasn't ready for a wife yet. He was still preparing me for my "wife-to-be" in His time, not mine.

One night, while worshiping with these fantastic Spirit-filled believers, I had an open vision. Jesus appeared and there was a big Santa Claus sack next to Him. He grabbed it with both hands and swung it over His shoulder. It appeared to be heavy because it seemed a chore picking it up and swinging it over His shoulder. Also, He was bent over while carrying it. He then looked at me with a big smile and said, "Follow Me."

The Jesus I've seen in my dreams and visions did not have perfectly manicured eyebrows. Jesus is a man's man. He looks more like the paintings I've seen of the laughing Jesus.

Jesus was reaffirming my call to do the work of ministry. This vision was yet another confirmation that I was called to the ministry. Although the sack was heavy, there would be joy in the work. The vision also reminds me to find joy in serving. The big smile on His face and the joy that radiated from Jesus was very infectious.

> *Come to Me, all you who labor and are heavy laden, and I will give you rest. Take My yoke upon you and learn from Me, for I am gentle and lowly in heart, and you will find rest for your souls. For My yoke is easy and My burden is light.*
> *~Matthew 11:28-30*

Jesus reassures us that the work He calls us to will be fulfilling. Our burden is light because He helps us carry it. Whatever He calls you to, He will empower you and bless the work of your hands. His joy will be your strength. You and I live for something bigger than ourselves; the Kingdom of God. Our purpose is to bring glory to God with everything we do.

> *It is not that we think we can do anything of lasting value by ourselves. Our only power and success come from God. He is the one who has enabled us to represent his new covenant. This is a covenant, not of written laws, but of the Spirit. The old way ends in death; in the new way, the Holy Spirit gives life.*
> *~2 Corinthians 3:5-6 NLT*

The three visions I decided to share with you were all open visions. Do you remember our four levels of vision? Each level is a higher revelation and becomes rarer.

1. Dreams, visions of the night
2. Visual pictures in your mind
3. Open visions outside of your mind. Although they are in front of you, you are still aware of your surroundings.

4. Trances, or being caught up in the vision. Being in a virtual reality vision, or being caught up to the third heaven is a higher form of experience and happens infrequently (see Acts 10:9-16 and Revelation 4:1-2)

A great example of an open vision in the Bible was when Jeremiah was watching a boiling caldron that was facing north. As he watched the steam rise up from the pot, God showed him the great army that would come from the North Country and lay siege to Jerusalem. His warnings of the coming Chaldean conquest and the subsequent Babylonian captivity would go unheeded (see Jeremiah 1:13-19).

"I'M TOO YOUNG FOR THIS"

As a Pastor, I like to supplement the church with special guest ministers, missionaries, and revivalists. I love hosting a good conference. Especially, Healing Conferences. At one such event, we had an evangelist who opened up his message that morning with a word of knowledge (see 1 Corinthians 12:7-11). This is knowing something by the Holy Spirit about someone, or some situation that he couldn't have known naturally. The word of knowledge the evangelist received included a vision.

He began to explain that early in the morning, as he was praying for the upcoming meeting, he saw a vision of a young woman (he stressed the word young) who was playing the keyboards but was experiencing a swollen wrist joint; possibly carpal tunnel. He saw her holding her hands out in front of her and while rotating her wrists she was heard saying, "I'm too young for this."

Immediately, my wife Nicole and I knew who this word of knowledge was for. Nicole had been training up a young woman, Amy, on the keyboards and in leading worship. Amy had been experiencing a swollen wrist joint to the point where the outer bone looked like a little golf ball. Once while playing with us on the worship team, she looked at us in frustration and rolled her wrist and said, "I'm too young for this." And, her last name is YOUNG! Nicole and I stared over at her sitting in the congregation and she had a look of surprise on her face. I yelled over at her and said, "Amy! That's for you!" She stood up with a look of shock on her face and when she did, the swelling on her wrist immediately disappeared. All pain was gone and she was instantly healed. Wow! Praise the Lord!

There have been many times that I have observed words of knowledge mixed with visual pictures given to people. When the person receiving the word of knowledge acknowledges it, a miracle or great encouragement follows.

THE VISION OF THE EMPTY CUPBOARDS

In the mid 1980's, when I was in my mid-twenties, I was asked to lead a home bible study. I was a fairly new believer but people sensed the spiritual leadership on me and wanted me to lead the group. One evening when we were ending our meeting in prayer, we were all griped by the Holy Spirit. We couldn't move on or end the meeting. An intercessory prayer burden came upon a woman in the group and she began to weep and pray in the Holy Spirit (tongues). She looked at me with tears in her eyes and told the group that she had a vision of empty cupboards and felt the worry of the parents who didn't know how they were going to feed their children.

I didn't know exactly what to do with this. I was fairly new to the whole Pentecostal/Charismatic experiences, so I simply asked everyone to pray for wisdom about what to do with this revelation.

SPIRIT WORLD

> *If any of you lacks wisdom, let him ask of God, who gives to all liberally and without reproach, and it will be given to him.*
> ~James 1:5

When we prayed, I thought of my neighbors. They were a young married couple with small children. I knew that he had lost his job recently and I was sure they needed help. We then decided to all pitch in some money, send someone to the grocery store, buy a bunch of food, and deliver it to their home. I was elected as the shopper and deliverer, and a young woman attending the group volunteered to help me. She claimed she could stretch a dollar like taffy; it turns out she could. We walked out of the grocery store with five bags of groceries. It was enough food to feed a family of four for over a week.

It was about 9:00 PM when we knocked on my neighbor's door. The husband and wife answered together. I explained that I was at a Bible study and we wanted to help somebody with groceries and that their family had come to my mind. The wife started to say "yes" but her husband's face was turning red and he said "no." He pulled his wife aside and whispered something to her and then came back to the door and assured us that they were all right and didn't need any help. He thanked us and sent us on our way.

Because I was new at being led by the Spirit I was a little dejected. I called my Pastor and relayed the whole story, concluding that the man's pride wouldn't allow him to accept the groceries. My Pastor assured me, "You can hear from God. Let's pray again for wisdom and then tell me what God shows you."

Well, God was faithful to bring to my mind a family in our church. I didn't know if they were going through any hardship or not, it was just a strong impression I had. I submitted this to my Pastor and he told me to bring the groceries to the Sunday morning service the next day.

I suggested that during the worship service I could slip out and put the groceries in their car without them knowing who had done it. He gave me the "okay." (I wasn't about to be rejected again because of someone's pride.)

During the worship service, I and a friend slipped outside into the parking lot and transferred all the groceries into the vehicle of the family that came to my mind the night before. (This was turning out to be kind of fun.) The following Sunday morning, the husband and wife whose car we slipped the groceries into the week before, stood up to give a testimony: "My union decided to go on strike a couple of weeks ago, and we were falling behind on our bills. My wife and I were getting very worried because our cupboards were empty and we have children to feed. We weren't sure we wanted to risk using gas to come to church last week, but we decided that nothing was going to stop us from worshiping our Lord. When we came out of church, we found our car full of groceries! We know that angels put them there! I go back to work this week and those groceries were the prefect amount to get us through!"

I turned to my friend who helped me put those groceries into their vehicle and said, "You are the strangest angel I ever saw." He responded back, "Speak for yourself." We had a good laugh.

Healing and spiritual gifts are imparted through prayer and the laying on of hands.

Chapter 8

SPIRITUAL IMPARTATION

For I long to see you, that I may impart to you some spiritual gift, so that you may be established. ~Romans 1:11

THE IMPARTATION OF GOD'S WORD

If we, as ministers of the Gospel, just preach and teach without the Holy Spirit imparting the grace needed to carry out the revelation, we are just putting a beast of burden on people. Along with good spiritual teaching there should be the spiritual impartation to carry it out. The Apostle Paul did not come to the churches with a good word of encouragement only. He came with the power and impartation of the Holy Spirit. Bible teaching can put people in legalistic bondage, or it can bring revelation, that when obeyed and implemented, can bring liberty.

The Word of God carries its own spiritual impartation. Jesus said that His words were "spirit and life" (see John 6:63). We must have confidence that when we share the Word of God, the enabling power of

SPIRIT WORLD

the Holy Spirit goes with it. I love this verse in the book of Isaiah where God says that His word will accomplish what He sends it forth to do.

> *For as the rain comes down, and the snow from heaven,*
> *And do not return there,*
> *But water the earth,*
> *And make it bring forth and bud,*
> *That it may give seed to the sower*
> *And bread to the eater,*
> *So shall My word be that goes forth from My mouth;*
> *It shall not return to Me void,*
> *But it shall accomplish what I please,*
> *And it shall prosper in the thing for which I sent it.*
> ~Isaiah 55:10-11

I have such faith in the spiritual impact of God's Word. I once felt inadequate to stand in front of people and teach the Bible. I told the Lord, "I have nothing. What wisdom could I possibly have that will help people?" The answer that came back kind of shocked me. This is how the Lord responded: "You're right, you don't have anything. It's the power of My Words and the anointing on your life that feeds people and sets them free." Wow, you mean it's not about me??? This actually set me free from thinking that I have to be profound. I just have to be faithful to preach the Word, and the spiritual impartation of that Word will help folks. This is the reason I put so much scripture in my Bible teaching. I am not coming with my own words; I'm coming with God's Word. I don't come quoting a lot of poems and song lyrics. I don't even bring a lot of quotes from famous celebrities or theologians. I don't come with comparative speculation and opinions of men. Only God's word can bring healing and salvation. Only the eternal promises of God can bring renewed hope to a weary soul. Paul told Timothy to preach the WORD!

Spiritual Impartation

> *I charge you therefore before God and the Lord Jesus Christ, who will judge the living and the dead at His appearing and His kingdom: Preach the word! Be ready in season and out of season. Convince, rebuke, exhort, with all longsuffering and teaching.* ~2 Timothy 4:1-2

I know that if preachers would start to preach the Word and not just a sentiment from their own heart, people would be greatly impacted. We must be convinced that only the Word of God has the power to turn a life around and set people free from demonic oppression.

> *I have not sent these prophets, yet they ran.*
> *I have not spoken to them, yet they prophesied.*
> *But if they had stood in My counsel,*
> *And had caused My people to hear My words,*
> *Then they would have turned them from their evil way*
> *And from the evil of their doings.* ~Jeremiah 23:21-22

The gospel was never meant to be dry sermonizing and philosophical principles. It was meant to carry the blast of heaven. The Word of God is the hammer that breaks the rock into pieces. It's the fire that burns off the dross with unquenchable heat. It's the soothing ointment for a wounded and broken soul.

> *For our gospel did not come to you in word only, but also in power, and in the Holy Spirit and in much assurance, as you know what kind of men we were among you for your sake.* ~1 Thessalonians 1:5

> *And my speech and my preaching were not with persuasive words of human wisdom, but in demonstration of the Spirit and of power, that your faith should not be in the wisdom of men but in the power of God.* ~1 Corinthians 2:4-5

IMPARTATION BY THE LAYING ON OF HANDS

Now Joshua the son of Nun was full of the spirit of wisdom, for Moses had laid his hands on him; so the children of Israel heeded him, and did as the LORD had commanded Moses.
~Deuteronomy 34:9

Moses knew it was time for him to die, and that Israel would need a new leader. Joshua the son of Nun had been Moses' assistant and military commander for over forty years. This was one long apprenticeship. Joshua was God's choice and possessed the giftings as a military general to lead the nation in the conquest of the land of Canaan. His natural giftings and years of training were not enough for the immense responsibility that was required. During the inauguration ceremony, Moses laid hands on Joshua to transfer spiritual gifting. The Bible says that an impartation of wisdom entered Joshua. It's awesome to think that through prayer and the laying on of hands, the spiritual gift of wisdom can be imparted (see 1 Corinthians 12:7-11).

The Bible teaches that when we as Christians pray and lay hands on people, there is a blessing that can be imparted. The book of Hebrews states that the doctrine of laying-on of hands is an elementary principle of Christ.

Therefore, leaving the discussion of the elementary principles of Christ, let us go on to perfection, not laying again the foundation of repentance from dead works and of faith toward God, of the doctrine of baptisms, of laying on of hands, of resurrection of the dead, and of eternal judgment.
~Hebrews 6:1-2

When Paul's disciple Timothy was set into his ministry, the elders laid hands on him and the Bible says that a spiritual gift was imparted to him. God transferred to young Timothy a powerful endowment to pastor and teach the Bible.

> *Do not neglect the gift that is in you, which was given to you by prophecy with the laying on of the hands of the eldership.*
> ~1 Timothy 4:14

When I was 22 years old, I traveled in a Christian rock band playing drums and ministering to young people my age. We not only did concerts but also led worship at many different functions and venues. One of these was a local chapter of an international women's group called "Women, Word and Worship" (WWW). I was playing my drums for the short worship set and didn't realize that the special speaker for the meeting was staring at me. At the end of worship, I got up from behind the drums wearing jeans, a leather jacket and straight, dishwater blond hair that was so long it nearly touched my rear end. As I walked over to my table to sit with my friends, this prominent minister called me out.

"Hey, you with the long hair and the leather jacket! I need you to come over here and let me pray and prophesy over you."

I didn't know what was going on. Was I about to be publicly rebuked? What sort of a strange thing is this? I stood up in front of the man and he proceeded to prophesy to me. "God has shown me that you are a strong-willed individual. You will keep going when others quit. You are going to need that characteristic because God has a ministry for you. For what the Lord has called you to, you're going to need to be bulldog stubborn and tenacious. Also, I feel that God wants me to do a transfer of anointing. I am going to take your hands and pray, and then God will impart an anointing (spiritual gift, or enablement). I very rarely do this. In fact, the Lord has only had me do this to one other person. Do you want this?"

I said "yes" but I had no idea what was going to happen, or what this all meant. With that, the prominent minister grabbed my hands and began to pray for me. I could literally feel energy coming from his hands into my hands, and running up my arms.

He asked me, "Do you feel that?"

"I sure do."

"How does it make you feel?"

"I feel like I want to run around the building a couple of times."

"Good. You're going to need that."

With that last comment, the brief ceremony was over and he continued on with a teaching. He acted all "matter-of-fact" about the whole thing, but I was left processing what just happened to me.

Years later, I was ministering in a church that was associated with this man's ministry. This minister who prayed for me was apostolic, and had many churches submitted to his association. After I had delivered a rousing, straightforward word, mixed with some light-hearted humor, people approached me. They commented that I reminded them of this particular minister. I related that he had laid hands on me some years prior. They told me that it was uncanny because I sounded just like him the way I ministered the word. I wasn't a carbon copy, but there were some powerful similarities.

After this experience I realized the power of impartation through the laying on of hands. I sought out many respected men and women of God and asked if they would please pray for me and impart some spiritual gift as the Lord wills. I have had prominent revival leaders lay hands on me. When I had a revivalist come to the church I was pastoring, I made sure I received prayer at some point before the meetings were over.

An older couple visited the church one Sunday and I discovered that they were vacationing at a local campground. I asked if I could visit their campsite later that day. I love sitting around the campfire conversing with folks. As my wife and I talked with them, we discovered that he was a direct descendent of Jonathan Edwards, the great revivalist preacher during the First Great Awakening in America just before the Revolutionary War. Then we discovered that his wife had been baptized by none other than Amie Simple McPherson. She was founder of the Foursquare Church and Pastor of Angelus Temple. She was very famous in the 1920's and 30's as a Pentecostal preacher and media celebrity. I immediately had them pray for us to impart some spiritual gift.

You may think I'm a little off my rocker but I believe what the Bible says about spiritual impartation and I've seen it proved out. When you realize that ministers carry with them spiritual giftings that you need, you will treat them with much more respect. You will honor the anointing on their lives. Remember what the Apostle Paul said to the Roman Church:

> *For I long to see you, that I may impart to you some spiritual gift, so that you may be established.* ~Romans 1:11

When I read my Bible, I challenge myself to believe it. Jesus told us that certain signs would follow those who believe. One of those signs would be that they would lay hands on the sick and they would recover (see Mark 16:17-18). I must admit, I don't always have faith for an instantaneous miracle when I pray for someone, but I always believe that they will begin to recover according to Mark 16:18. God will reverse whatever curse has come upon them. Instead of getting worse and worse, they will get better and better. I believe that healing virtue flows through the believer in Christ. It's not always a matter of whether I feel anything. We pray for the sick by faith. *"And the prayer of faith will save the sick" (James 5:15a).* A healing is different from a miracle. A healing is a gradual recovery and a miracle is instantaneous. Many times when folks are prayed for, they don't sense an instantaneous miracle so they're not sure they received anything. When you are prayed for, believe that you will recover based on God's Word. *"…they shall lay hands on the sick and they SHALL RECOVER" (Mark 16:18)*. I have to tell you, it's just as miraculous when God causes a terminal illness to go into remission as it is if you were instantaneously healed. We must believe that when we as Christians lay hands and pray for people, God is going to do something.

I was managing a fast food restaurant and a woman employee began crying quietly. I asked if everything was all right. She told me, "I am in pain and sick but I can't afford to go home or take any time off. I'm a single mother and have to provide for my children."

This really broke my heart and compassion rose up in me. I told her that I was a Christian and believed that God can heal people. I asked her if I could lay my hand on her shoulder and pray in the name of Jesus for God to heal her. She agreed and as I prayed briefly, I could feel the loving, mighty presence of God come upon her. The tears really started to flow now and she started jumping up and down in the back of the restaurant yelling, "The pain is gone! Jesus has healed me! Thank you so much for praying for me. No one has ever asked to pray for me before."

I must admit, when she told me that no one had ever asked to pray with her before, I had to fight back some of my own tears. I was so happy that God met her and showed His love for her. She began telling all the other employees that if they ever got sick to let me pray for them and God would heal them.

Lay hands and pray for people with faith and watch what God does.

GOD TOOK THE SPIRIT ON MOSES AND IMPARTED IT TO 70 ELDERS

Then the LORD came down in the cloud, and spoke to him, and took of the Spirit that was upon him, and placed the same upon the seventy elders; and it happened, when the Spirit rested upon them, that they prophesied, although they never did so again. ~Numbers 11:25

This experience foreshadowed the day of Pentecost in the book of Acts, chapter 2. Moses needed help in leading the children of Israel to the Promised Land. God took of the Spirit that empowered Moses to lead and distributed it to 70 elders. The sign that the Spirit came upon those elders was that they prophesied. In Acts chapter 2, the Spirit that was on Jesus was transferred to the church. The outward sign was that they spoke in tongues and prophesied. Now the church is spiritually empowered to carry out the works of Christ.

God still miraculously imparts to people today. You don't always have to have someone lay hands on you. God is sovereign and if He wants to take an anointing from someone and give it to someone else, that's His business. He doesn't need permission. All anointings and giftings belong to Him and He can distribute them as He chooses.

I was asked to go to a special training meeting for ministers. I still remember the title of the seminar: "97 Reasons Why Ministries Fail." I kid you not! As the lecture droned on, my mind was jolted back into focus as the speaker yelled out the next point, "Number 22!" Somewhere between 22 and 97, the speaker mentioned that there were 22 churches currently in the Michigan District of the Assemblies of God that did not have a pastor. He said, "God is calling some of you to step up and take responsibility of one of these churches." Immediately, I sensed the Holy Spirit nudge my spirit and tell me that I was supposed to step up and pastor one of those churches. I hadn't been a senior pastor up to that point.

I began to argue a little bit with God on this. I didn't feel qualified. I wasn't sure I wanted the responsibility. I told the Holy Spirit that I would be the 98th example of why ministries fail. I had a lot of fun being a youth pastor, or assistant pastor. I could give suggestions and advice to the senior pastor and if it went bad it was the pastor's fault, not mine. I had pulled knives out of the backs of pastors I served (figuratively speaking). I had seen pastors betrayed, lied about, and defamed in many colorful, assorted ways. And worst of all, they sometimes had to confront people about their sin. Oh man, I'm not sure I was having any of that. When people are corrected about anything, their true colors are revealed. Sometimes beautiful hues of humility would emerge; sometimes grotesque shades of rebellious specters would manifest.

The Holy Spirit began to reason with me, "I have prepared you. You have enough experience and education. I will be with you." Even with all these assurances I still felt inadequate. I then looked up at the seminar leader. I was not listening to his points anymore, but was aware of him speaking. It was like a Charlie Brown cartoon; when the adults talk to the children, you can't make out the words, all you hear is "Mwa-mwa, mwa… wah-wah, wah-wah." Then, a spiritual Bengal Tiger came out of the man lecturing and ran around the circumference of the building. As it circled the outside walls inside the auditorium, the tiger headed straight for me and ran right inside of me. The Holy Spirit then spoke to me and said, "There is an anointing to be a courageous pastor, now you have no excuse."

God knows how to equip you for what He has called you to do. You are called by God, and not by man. You have a unique call and purpose.

He has good works for you to do. God will find a way to impart spiritual gifts to you.

> *For we are His workmanship, created in Christ Jesus for good works, which God prepared beforehand that we should walk in them.* ~Ephesians 2:10

IMPARTATION FROM THE ATMOSPHERE

> *Then Saul sent messengers to take David. And when they saw the group of prophets prophesying, and Samuel standing as leader over them, the Spirit of God came upon the messengers of Saul, and they also prophesied. And when Saul was told, he sent other messengers, and they prophesied likewise. Then Saul sent messengers again the third time, and they prophesied also.* ~1 Samuel 19:20-21

What was happening there? This is what I call a "God Zone." The Spirit of God was so strong around Samuel and his group of prophets that whenever anyone came into close proximity, they too got caught up in the atmosphere and began to prophecy. This is what happens in a revival atmosphere. God's presence is so strong in the meetings that you become swept up in the strong current of revival and imparted with blessings.

Have you ever been in a church meeting where the spirit of wisdom and revelation fell and everyone received incredible insight from God (see Ephesians 1:15-17)? How about when the atmosphere is charged with a prophetic anointing and everyone gets prophetic revelation? Even folks who have never prophesied before are inspired to give a prophetic word or share some revelation from the Bible.

SPIRIT WORLD

Have you ever been in a service when a powerful healing virtue fell and people received healing so easily? This happened in the ministry of Jesus when a healing presence would manifest in His meeting.

> *Now it happened on a certain day, as He was teaching, that there were Pharisees and teachers of the law sitting by, who had come out of every town of Galilee, Judea, and Jerusalem.* **And the power of the Lord was present to heal them.**
>
> ~Luke 5:17

There have been tremendous revivals where a God Zone was created and all who went on a pilgrimage to these locations soaked up the revival atmosphere. In the mid 1990's, there was a powerful revival that broke out in the Toronto Airport Church in Toronto, Canada.

I had heard about the outpouring, and a group of friends wanted my wife and I to join them on a trip to see what was happening there. I was excited to see Toronto; I had never been there before and I love a good road trip. On the way my friends began warning me about the strange manifestations that had occurred during the revival. They didn't want me to be freaked out. I assured them that I had been in Charismatic circles long enough to see all kinds of weirdness. They explained that some folks would shake violently under the power; others would be lying on their backs on the floor, weeping and rocking back and forth. They reported that when the Spirit of God falls in a meeting it can seem like mass pandemonium. This revival was not a man-made, man controlled, ordered event; it was a holy mess. I responded with, "I don't care how high you jump, or how loud you shout, it's how straight you walk once you leave the meeting. Are people's lives changed for the better? Is there good fruit from what people are experiencing?"

I have to say, even though my friends had prepared me it still felt like a runaway train ride. There is a sound to revival, and I have since

Spiritual Impartation

learned to recognize that sound. It's the sound of people being touched by God in a deep and profound way; it's the sound of people being set free. There is a glory in the worship music and in the preaching and teaching of God's word. When the atmosphere of heaven collides with the atmosphere of this earth there is tremendous upheaval. Using natural weather systems as a metaphor, when warm air streams collide with cold air fronts, tornados can result. The atmosphere from heaven can bring fabulous peace, or it will rock your world with a vortex of power.

We were only able to attend three of the revival meetings. After each meeting I waited to receive prayer. Small prayer teams of three or four would work their way through the disorganized prayer lines. Finally, a prayer group reached me and leading the group was an elderly lady who prayed very fervently. When she began praying for me I began to weep. It felt like a weeping of intercession and repentance mixed. Then I felt a breakthrough and victory. Joy swept over me and I wanted to laugh and shout. If I shouted in that environment no one would have noticed. Lots of people were shouting, laughing, crying, or whatever. At the end of all three meetings that I attended, I waited for a prayer team. When they prayed for me the same experience happened. First, I would weep, sense a release and victory, and then I would experience joy. I didn't think much of the experiences at first, but while processing the overall visit to the Toronto Revival I did think it was odd that the same pattern of experience happened to me three times.

On the way home I was asked if I received anything from the revival. I told everyone that I really didn't know if I received anything. At the time I was a Youth Pastor and the next Sunday at our church our Pastor explained to everyone that my wife, Nicole, and I had visited the Toronto revival (also known as the Toronto Blessing, or the Father's Blessing). He believed that we had received an impartation from the revival and wanted all the youth and young adults to come up front for prayer. About fifteen students responded to the call to come up front for prayer. As Nicole and I began praying for the students, they began to cry and weep, some very loudly. After that they experienced a release and then a joy. The joy was so strong on three of them that they started laughing uncontrollably. They were really laughing hard. It was kind of awkward. I mean, you could sense that it was God but you didn't know how the Pastor or the folks in the church were going to react. What was even more strange is that these young people were not given to extravagant outbursts. They were not drama junkies or attention hounds. A public display like this would not happen from these unlikely candidates. The Pastor was sensitive to the Spirit and knew this was God so he allowed it to continue. In fact, he preached over the top of the students, who were laughing loudly. It was great!

The same pattern that happened to me at the Toronto revival happened to these students that I prayed for. First, they wept, and then experienced a victory and joy. God taught me something that day about impartation from an atmosphere of revival. God caused that pattern to be repeated so I would put things together and see that we are imparted with spiritual blessings when we are in a revival atmosphere. We become carriers of revival. What is imparted to us, we can in turn impart to others. You cannot give something you don't possess. You cannot give grace if you have not received grace. You cannot release refreshing from the presence of the Lord unless you are filled. My advice to you would be to attend meetings where God shows up in power. You will become a carrier of greater glory. God will open up opportunities for you to bless others. Out of our hearts should flow rivers of living water (see John 7:38). Don't let your river of blessing be stopped up. Get into God's refreshing presence and let the river flow.

IMPARTATION BY ASSOCIATION

He who walks with wise men will be wise,
But the companion of fools will be destroyed.   ~Proverbs 13:20

Our associations define us. What kind of people are drawn to you? Who are your inner circle of friends? The old saying that "birds of a feather flock together" is generally true. The Bible teaches that there is an impartation from your associations. There is a positive and negative to this. It is possible to be more intentional about the kind of people we let into our inner circle. The Bible wouldn't give us warnings and wisdom about the influence of association if you didn't have a choice. God has given us discernment to choose the good and reject the bad.

By nature, I am an extroverted person. I have always made friends easily. In many cases I have been very aggressive in seeking out friends. In my curiosity to know people I have experienced the full spectrum of friends. I have had friends that cause a spontaneous chemical reaction of craziness. There were certain people I would get together with, and a wild look would come over our eyes; we were capable of outlandish things. As fun as some of those relationships were, random acts of wildness are childish, and in some cases could mean prison time or serious bodily injury.

I have had other relationships that were very toxic. I have always tried to be a devoted friend. I always felt that a true friend stayed with you through good times and bad. I still feel this way. But what happens when you are trying to save a drowning person and they are fighting you so hard that you risk being drowned with them? At what point do you release them to their own devices because they are bent on self-destruction and they don't care who goes down with them? Like Kryptonite to Superman, you can literally feel the life force being

SPIRIT WORLD

sucked out of you every time you're around this type of person. They have become a black hole with such a powerful gravitational pull that light itself turns black as it's sucked into the vortex of their pain and self-destructive obsession. When you come to the realization that you're not the one to help them because they are dragging you down with them into their self-destructive pit of hopeless despair, run away! Run away!

Do not be deceived: "Evil company corrupts good habits."
~1 Corinthians 15:33

This verse couldn't be clearer. If you forsake the fellowship of the saints and are always associating with those who do not know Christ, they will eventually corrupt you. You are not smarter than God. You are not wiser than God's word. If you think that being around people who do not know God will not affect you eventually, you are deceived. Whenever a Bible verse begins with the phrase "Do not be deceived," you would do well to take heed.

A Pastor came to visit one of his faithful parishioners who hadn't come to church for several weeks. He knocked on the door and from inside he heard a low voice. "Come in Pastor and have a seat." Inside, the fire was going strong in the hearth and there were two comfortable chairs angled toward the fire with a coffee table in between. The man who hadn't been to church for several weeks sat in one of the chairs and stared into the flames. The Pastor sat in the other chair and immediately enjoyed the radiant heat that emanated from the glow. Neither spoke. As they sat transfixed by the dancing embers, the Pastor grabbed the poker leaning next to the hearth. There in the fire was a glowing coal about the size of a man's hand. The Pastor separated it from the flames to a place by itself. It didn't take long for the separated coal to cease its orange glow and grow cold. Still, there were no words spoken and the Pastor got up, put his coat back on, and headed toward the door. The man never got up from his chair. He turned his head toward the front door as the Pastor was about to leave and said, "Thank you for the sermon Pastor, I'll see you next Sunday."

The Bible tells us not to be yoked together with unbelievers (see 2 Corinthians 6:14-18), and yet, how will we influence people with our friendships if we are to be separated? I think the balance is in a question we should ask ourselves: Who is influencing who? If we find ourselves in relationships where we are being influenced negatively, then we need to take inventory. Don't make yourself so available to folks who are constantly bringing you down and causing you to compromise your walk with God. Jesus was a friend of sinners but He didn't become one (see Matthew 11:19). He was the influencer. He brought with Him the atmosphere of heaven and lives around Him were changed and transformed. He commissioned us to do the same.

> *Now when they saw the boldness of Peter and John, and perceived that they were uneducated and untrained men, they marveled. And they realized that they had been with Jesus.*
> ~Acts 4:13-14

Being with Jesus will change you. You, in turn, will change the lives of those around you. We can be the influencers instead of being overcome by the wicked values of the world. Maintain your private relationship with Him and it will be seen outwardly. I have to stay in the Word of God every day. I can tell when I have neglected my private devotional time because of the busyness of life. I love the Lord, and I love hearing from Him. God speaks to me while I'm reading my Bible. It never fails. There is always something in my daily Bible reading that stands out. God promises to show us great and mighty things that we do not know.

> *Call to Me, and I will answer you, and show you great and mighty things, which you do not know.* ~Jeremiah 33:3

SPIRIT WORLD

There are manifold blessings for those who watch daily at the gates of wisdom. What is done in secret will be rewarded openly. For our faith to grow we must feed it. The food for our faith is the Word of God (see Romans 10:17).

> *Blessed is the man who listens to me,*
> *Watching daily at my gates,*
> *Waiting at the posts of my doors.*
> *For whoever finds me finds life,*
> *And obtains favor from the LORD.* ~Proverbs 8:34-35

I love being around people who have a spirit of faith. Their love for the Lord and His Word is infectious. I always leave their presence feeling built up and feeling like I can do anything. All things are possible for those who believe (see Mark 9:23). Joshua was Moses' assistant for forty years and the same spirit of faith that was on Moses was imparted to Joshua. Elisha was the assistant of Elijah for fourteen years and received a double portion of faith (see 2 Kings 2:9)

> *And since we have the same spirit of faith, according to what is written, "I believed and therefore I spoke," we also believe and therefore speak.* ~2 Corinthians 4:13

King David had that same spirit of faith. He had a "can do" attitude. He believed in the God of the impossible. When he was on the run from jealous King Saul, all of the indebted and disgruntled gathered themselves to him.

> *And everyone who was in distress, everyone who was in debt, and everyone who was discontented gathered to him. So he became captain over them. And there were about four hundred men with him.* ~1 Samuel 22:2

Because of their association with King David they became mighty men. That spirit of faith that was on David was imparted to these men and their exploits as warriors became legendary (see 2 Samuel 23:8-23). A transformation will take place in your life as you spend time with Jesus and people of faith.

I want to recap this teaching on spiritual impartation. Here are the four ways you will be imparted with amazing blessings to advance the Kingdom of God and live victoriously.

1. **The Word of God** imparts life to us
2. **The laying on of hands** will bring a spiritual impartation to us. We are to lay hands on the sick and they will recover. Healing and spiritual gifts are imparted through prayer and the laying on of hands.
3. **An atmosphere of revival** will impart a spiritual blessing to you.
4. **Your associations** will impart spiritually to you. Intentionally make friends with people of faith.

Now concerning spiritual gifts (charismata), brethren, I do not want you to be ignorant.

Chapter 9

WHY DO THEY SPEAK IN TONGUES?

And they were all filled with the Holy Spirit and began to speak with other tongues, as the Spirit gave them utterance.
                                                    ~Acts 2:4

I was 18 years old when I landed a job with General Motors. We called it "Generous Motors" because they paid so well and provided great benefits for their employees. In Saginaw Michigan, where I lived, General Motors was the largest employer by far. The factory in which I worked was called Saginaw Metal Castings Plant, also known as Saginaw Grey Iron. It was the largest metal casting factory in the world. It employed over six thousand people in 1978-79. It was like a little city inside this massive multileveled structure. There were even street names for inside navigation. It was so loud inside that most people wore ear plugs. Fork trucks, little cranes and golf carts pulling trailers buzzed around all the time. The clanking sounds of machinery mixed with the smell and orange glow of molten iron being poured into sandstone molds filled your senses. It was a beehive of movement and energy. In

SPIRIT WORLD

some ways, the atmosphere was invigorating. For an 18 year old young man it was a little scary and intimidating at first.

Have you ever felt alone in a crowd? I was in this huge cafeteria looking for someplace to sit down and I spotted some guys praying over their food. I thought, "Well that looks like a safe group over there, I will go and sit by them." Over a short period of time I became friends with one of the guys and he invited me to his church. I took him up on the offer and went with him to a mid-week service.

It was a typical looking small church. When you first walked in, there was a small foyer and the bathrooms were off to the side. When you went into the sanctuary, there were pews that could seat approximately sixty people. There was a raised platform with a pulpit in front and center, and traditional church hanging lights. It was not an elaborate rich church, but it was practical and functional.

The pastor was a friendly middle-aged man. He was dressed casually; I assumed it was because it was a mid-week service and not a Sunday morning. The Pastor took charge of the meeting and stood in front of the pulpit on the raised platform. So far everything appeared as I expected, pretty normal. The Pastor assumed what I call 'the Lutheran prayer stance'; hands folded in front of his body with palms facing in, knees slightly bent and shoulders relaxed. When prayer begins, you are supposed to close your eyes and lower your head to where your chin almost touches your chest.

The pastor said that he wanted to open the service with some intercession (a pastor word for prayer). He went on to explain different needs within the church that needed prayer attention and then said, "let's begin." I started to assume the Lutheran prayer stance when things went nuts. Just as my chin almost touched my chest, my friend started wailing in some foreign language and then went to his knees. I heard people praying loudly in a cacophony of foreign languages all around me. (I am sure that was what it sounded like at the tower of Babel [see Genesis 11:1-9].) No one warned me about this, nor explained anything to me. I had no idea what was going on. I found out later that they were "praying in tongues." I didn't even know there was such a thing as "praying in tongues." I was thoroughly freaked out! What was happening!?

My survival instincts kicked in and I knew I should play it cool. I didn't know what kind of strange religious cult I had stumbled into, but I knew that eventually they would let us leave and then I would never come back again. But until the meeting was dismissed I decided to blend in by praying the Lord's prayer under my breath (also known as the "Our Father" prayer found in Matthew 6:9-13).

After the initial "shock and awe" of my first experience with people speaking in tongues, I didn't just dismiss it. I found out that speaking in tongues was actually in the New Testament of the Bible; the same Bible in our bookshelf at home. If speaking in tongues was in the Bible, and practiced by the early believers of the church, then I wondered why my church didn't promote speaking in tongues. If the spiritual gift of tongues is legit, is there a right and wrong way to use the gift? I realize that when most people have a bad or uncomfortable experience, they tend to avoid a future repeat. Apparently, I am an exception to the rule because I wanted to understand what the heck just happened.

The first thing I came to understand was that the word "tongues" is an old English word for languages. So speaking in tongues, in the old English sense, is speaking in a known or foreign language. The Greek language is much more descriptive and precise at times. There are two Greek words that are translated into our English word "language" or "tongue." One is "dialektos" (Strong's #1258, see Acts 2:6). This is where we get the English word "dialect". When this word is used, it refers to a language that you learn naturally by studying it. The second Greek word is "glossolalia" (Strong's #1100, see Acts 2:4). When this word is used, it refers to speaking in tongues; speaking a language that you have NOT learned naturally. You are speaking by the Holy Spirit. Wow!

You are not supposed to understand with your mind what you are praying in tongues. Your spirit is praying with the assistance of the Holy Spirit. This way, the Holy Spirit can bypass your mind. You and I are not always capable of comprehending with our limited understanding what needs to be prayed. We don't always know how to pray. We are not capable of articulating and framing into words what's on the mind of the Spirit. Thank God I can pray with the help of the Holy Spirit (pray in tongues)! I don't always know how to pray, or what to pray, but the Holy Spirit does. There are times I get an intense burden to pray but I don't fully understand what is going on in the spiritual realm. Thank God that at times like that I can pray in tongues.

> *For he who speaks in a tongue does not speak to men but to God, for no one understands him; however, in the spirit he speaks mysteries.* ~1 Corinthians 14:2

> *For if I pray in a tongue, my spirit prays, but my understanding is unfruitful. What is the conclusion then? I will pray with the spirit, and I will also pray with the understanding. I will sing with the spirit, and I will also sing with the understanding.* ~1 Corinthians 14:14-15

THE MAN-MADE DOCTRINE OF CESSATIONISM

Whenever I used to hear the word "doctrine" I would feel blunted by the club of religiosity. My mind would conjure up images of monks down in a candle lit cellar copying ancient manuscripts. Or, I would think of a harsh Bible thumping old man in a black suit that believes God lives in the "no-fun zone" and if you get any enjoyment from anything it must be sinful. I later learned that the word "doctrine" simply means "teaching." A Bible doctrine is a teaching on a subject in the Bible.

Amazingly enough, not all Bible doctrines are biblical, or based on the Bible. Some are man-made distortions. Some are outright demonic. Others are God-given teachings that bloom out of the Bible and will bring life. There are three different types of doctrine: doctrines of demons, doctrines made up by men and doctrines from God.

1. **Doctrines of demons:**

   Now the Spirit expressly says that in latter times some will depart from the faith, giving heed to deceiving spirits and doctrines of demons, speaking lies in hypocrisy, having their own conscience seared with a hot iron. ~1 Timothy 4:1-2

2. **Doctrines of men:**

   And in vain they worship Me, teaching as doctrines the commandments of men. ~Matthew 15:9

3. **Doctrines of God:**

   Jesus answered them and said, "My doctrine is not Mine, but His who sent Me. If anyone wills to do His will, he shall know concerning the doctrine, whether it is from God or whether I speak on My own authority. ~John 7:16-17

So, just to reiterate the three different types of doctrine, there are doctrines of demons, doctrines manufactured by men, and doctrines that are from God that spring forth from the Bible and bring life. Just because someone dresses up a teaching with religious ribbons and fifty-dollar theological terms, doesn't necessarily mean they have rightly divided the word of God. Some have good hearts and are just repeating what they have been taught. Others are purposely twisting and contorting the

SPIRIT WORLD

Bible to justify their unbelief. Our job is not to always judge men's hearts but to discern truth from error.

What is the "Doctrine of Cessationism?" It is a man-made teaching that believes "tongues" and all miraculous demonstrations of the Holy Spirit, including prophecy and divine healing, have ceased. They believe that when the New Testament books were completed, and the first century Apostles died, the miraculous gifts and demonstrations of the Holy Spirit (see 1 Corinthians 12:7-11) were no longer needed.

I knew nothing of this, or that the church I was raised in believed this. Right after my experience with my friend's tongue-talking church, I began asking questions. Of course, I asked my mother because mothers know everything. Right?

"Hey Mom, how come our church doesn't speak in tongues? It's in the Bible." She told me that once the New Testament was written we didn't need tongues, prophecy, or the other miraculous demonstration of the Spirit. My response was, "Can you show me in the Bible where it says those gifts will cease once the Bible is written?" She then took me to 1 Corinthians, chapter 13.

> *Love never fails. But whether there are prophecies, they will fail; whether there are tongues, they will cease; whether there is knowledge, it will vanish away. For we know in part and we prophesy in part. But when that which is perfect has come, then that which is in part will be done away. When I was a child, I spoke as a child, I understood as a child, I thought as a child; but when I became a man, I put away childish things. For now we see in a mirror, dimly, but then face to face. Now I know in part, but then I shall know just as I also am known. And now abide faith, hope, love, these three; but the greatest of these is love.* ~1 Corinthians 13:8-13

Why do They Speak in Tongues?

As I read this portion of the Bible, having no theological training at that time, it seemed to me that there was nothing in this passage about these gifts passing away once the Bible was completed. That's because it's not THERE. It seemed to me that tongues and prophecy will cease, or pass away, when we are face to face with Christ, at His Second Coming. When we have glorified bodies, and are in the presence of God almighty, why would we need tongues and prophecy? We will have a perfect understanding. We will be spiritually capable of comprehending spiritual things that may be a little out of reach for us now.

Scripture tells us that spiritual gifts are intended to continue until the Second Coming of Christ (see 1 Corinthians 12:7-11).

> *I thank my God always concerning you for the grace of God which was given to you by Christ Jesus, that you were enriched in everything by Him in all utterance and all knowledge, even as the testimony of Christ was confirmed in you, so that you come short in no gift, eagerly waiting for the revelation of our Lord Jesus Christ, who will also confirm you to the end, that you may be blameless in the day of our Lord Jesus Christ.*
> ~1 Corinthians 1:4-8

It is the Apostle Paul's desire that we do not come short in any gift (Greek, charismata, grace gift), as we wait for the return, or revelation of Christ. This word for gift is the same word used to describe the grace gifts of the Holy Spirit in 1 Corinthians 12-14. These gifts include tongues, prophecy, discerning of spirits, working of miracles, faith, words of wisdom and knowledge, and gifts of healing. Do we still need supernatural faith? How about wisdom, knowledge and healing? Besides, why would God gives us instruction in His word about these gifts of the Spirit and their use if we weren't going to need them? Why would He encourage us to desire them fervently?

SPIRIT WORLD

> *Now concerning spiritual gifts (charismata), brethren, I do not want you to be ignorant.* ~1 Corinthians 12:1

> *Pursue love, and desire spiritual gifts (charismata), but especially that you may prophesy.* ~1 Corinthians 14:1

To conclude, you most certainly can categorize the doctrine of Cessationism as a man-made doctrine because it distorts the scripture and misleads. I would also say it is a devilish doctrine because it robs people of the power of God. We are at war with the powers of darkness. You don't bring a knife to a gun fight, and you don't fight a spiritual battle unless you have powerful spiritual weapons. Why not desire ALL that God has for us? Including tongues. If it is beneficial why put it on a shelf?

> *For the weapons of our warfare are not carnal but mighty in God for pulling down strongholds.* ~2 Corinthians 10:4

> *But know this, that in the last days perilous times will come: For men will be lovers of themselves... having a form of godliness but denying its power. And from such people turn away!* ~2 Timothy 3:1-2, 5

THE BAPTISM IN THE HOLY SPIRIT

> *I indeed baptize you with water unto repentance, but He who is coming after me is mightier than I, whose sandals I am not worthy to carry. He will baptize you with the Holy Spirit and fire.* ~Matthew 3:11

> *[5] For John truly baptized with water, but you shall be baptized with the Holy Spirit not many days from now.*
> *[8] But you shall receive power when the Holy Spirit has come*

upon you; and you shall be witnesses to Me in Jerusalem, and in all Judea and Samaria, and to the end of the earth.
~Acts 1:5, 8

A friend invited me to his Pentecostal church, and he had changed so much that I secretly wondered if he was in some religious cult. He didn't want to get drunk anymore. He was always happy. He was constantly talking about Jesus and the Bible. Come on… who does this? Nobody in their right mind WANTS to go to church, let alone invite all their friends to come along with them.

He caught me in a bad state; I was in a very low place. Not only was I recovering from a terrible car accident where I broke my jaw in seven places, but I was questioning everything at the time; the existence of God, heaven, hell and life after death. My life was a mess and I was greatly depressed. I thought to myself, "What could it hurt to check out his church?" So, I accepted his invitation.

Toward the end of the church service, the preacher gave an appeal to the people, "It's time for you to stop playing games with God. He has been appealing to you for several years. It's time to make your peace with him and ask Jesus to be your personal Lord and Savior. If you want to commit your life to Christ, and become His follower, then you need to get up out of your seat and come down to the front. You must be bold and come down to this altar right now. If you are ashamed to stand up for Jesus in front of these people who love you and want to see you grow in your relationship with God, how will you ever be able to stand up for Christ out in the world? Jesus said, 'For whoever is ashamed of Me and My words, of him the Son of Man will be ashamed when He comes in His own glory, and in His Father's, and of the holy angels'" (Luke 9:26).

I was sweating bullets. It was like the preacher was speaking directly to me. I was that person who was playing games and living a lukewarm

SPIRIT WORLD

commitment to God (Jesus said in Revelation 3:16 & 17, *"I know your works, that you are neither cold nor hot. I could wish you were cold or hot. So then, because you are lukewarm, and neither cold nor hot, I will vomit you out of My mouth."*)

As I sat there and wrestled with whether I should take the plunge and go up to receive Christ, I heard the still small voice of God, "If you don't go up front right now and commit your life to Me, your heart will become so hardened that you will not be able to hear Me calling you anymore."

I knew that impression had to be God speaking to me. What He said frightened me; I had been hardening my heart to the call of God for so long that I was dangerously close to shutting God out forever. I told the Lord that this was it, no more games, I was giving my life completely to Him and I would do whatever He wanted, even if it meant going to Zimbabwe (I didn't know where Zimbabwe was, but I was willing to go there). I even to told God I would believe everything in the Bible, INCLUDING TONGUES. I immediately got up and went down the aisle.

The preacher asked a guy, who was about my age, to pray with me. He led me in a prayer of repentance and I asked Jesus to be my personal Lord and Savior. After that he asked me if I would like to be baptized in the Holy Spirit. He was not talking about water baptism; this was a baptism into the Holy Spirit and power. He said it was God's will for every believer to be filled with the Spirit.

> *Therefore do not be unwise, but understand what the will of the Lord is. And do not be drunk with wine, in which is dissipation; but* **be filled with the Spirit.**   ~Ephesians 5:17-18

Why do They Speak in Tongues?

> *Then Peter said to them, "Repent, and let every one of you be baptized in the name of Jesus Christ for the remission of sins; and you shall receive the **gift of the Holy Spirit**. For the promise is to you and to your children, **and to all who are afar off, as many as the Lord our God will call."*   ~Acts 2:38-39

He told me that he was going to lay hands on me and lead me in a prayer to ask Jesus to fill me with the Holy Spirit and then I would start speaking in tongues. Speaking in tongues would be the outward evidence that I was baptized in the Spirit.

> **And they were all filled with the Holy Spirit** *and began to speak with other tongues, as the Spirit gave them utterance.*
> ~Acts 2:4

I just told God, back in my chair, that I would even receive TONGUES! Wow…and here was this guy asking me if I wanted to be filled with the Holy Spirit and speak in tongues. Well, we prayed but I couldn't speak in tongues. I didn't know what went wrong. The young guy at the altar told me to keep seeking and learning and eventually I would get it. I was so excited about my new life with Jesus that I shelved the whole "tongues" thing. I figured I would learn more and eventually I would be filled with the Holy Spirit.

I was determined to have all that God had for me. I knew that God shows no favoritism or partiality (see Acts 10:34 and Romans 2:11). He wouldn't allow some to be baptized in the Holy Spirit and speak in tongues, and say no to others. He said in His word, *"For the promise is to you and to your children, and to all who are afar off, as many as the Lord our God will call" (Acts 2:39)*. Either this was the will of God for everyone, or it was the will of God for no one.

As I studied, I learned that there is an experience beyond salvation. It's called the "Baptism in the Holy Spirit." Both Jesus and John the

SPIRIT WORLD

Baptist called this experience being "baptized with the Holy Spirit" (see Matthew 3:11 and Acts 1:5). When you receive it, you receive power to be a witness and live a better life. It is the gateway to the supernatural and to experiencing more fully the powerful gifts of the Holy Spirit (see 1 Corinthians 12:7-11). The outward physical evidence that you have been baptized in the Spirit is that you get to speak in tongues. Wow, you are downloaded with a heavenly language to pray with and use for your private devotion.

The book of Acts records the experience of being baptized in the Holy Spirit five times (see Acts 2:4, 8:14-18, 9:17, 10:44-46 and 19:6). Three times it specifically mentions the outward sign of tongues manifesting (see Acts 2:4, 10:44-46 and 19:6). When Ananias laid hands on Paul to receive the Holy Spirit (see Acts 9:17), the scripture does not state that he spoke in tongues. But we know that he did because Paul said in his letter to the Corinthians, *"I thank my God I speak with tongues more than you all." (1 Corinthians 14:18).* Another time tongues are not mentioned specifically is when the Samaritans were being prayed for to be filled with the Holy Spirit. When Peter and James laid hands on the Samaritans the effects were visibly seen by Simon the sorcerer (see Acts 8:17-18). Peter and John were not sent to Samaria for these people to receive Christ, or to be baptized in water. They had already experienced salvation and water baptism. Peter and John prayed for them that they might be filled with the Holy Spirit. Simon the sorcerer saw some power outwardly displayed that provoked him to want to control this power. To be totally consistent with the rest of the book of Acts, we would have to conclude that those Samaritan believers spoke in tongues and magnified God when they were filled with the Holy Spirit.

Why do They Speak in Tongues?

When Peter heard the household of Cornelius begin to speak in tongues, he concluded that this was the outward sign that they had been baptized in the Holy Spirit.

> *While Peter was still speaking these words, the Holy Spirit fell upon all those who heard the word. And those of the circumcision who believed were astonished, as many as came with Peter, because the gift of the Holy Spirit had been poured out on the Gentiles also. For they heard them speak with tongues and magnify God. Then Peter answered, "Can anyone forbid water, that these should not be baptized who have received the Holy Spirit just as we have?"* ~Acts 10:44-48

When Peter was relating this story to the Jerusalem council, he referred to that which was experienced by the household of Cornelius as being baptized with the Holy Spirit.

> *And as I began to speak, the Holy Spirit fell upon them, as upon us at the beginning. Then I remembered the word of the Lord, how He said, 'John indeed baptized with water, but you shall be baptized with the Holy Spirit.' If therefore God gave them the same gift as He gave us when we believed on the Lord Jesus Christ, who was I that I could withstand God?"* ~Acts 11:15-17

To be scripturally accurate, we must conclude that speaking in tongues is the outward physical evidence of receiving the Holy Spirit baptism. If we fail to see this, we may come to some false conclusions in the book of Acts.

1. **False conclusion #1:** The Holy Spirit baptism is receiving the Holy Spirit at salvation. To be true to the scriptures, you do receive the Holy Spirit at salvation; Romans 8:9 states, *"But you are not in the flesh but in the Spirit, if indeed the Spirit of God dwells in you. Now if anyone does not have the Spirit of Christ, he is not*

His." When a person asks Jesus to be their Lord and Savior, the Spirit of Christ (the Holy Spirit) indwells them. The Holy Spirit baptism is something more than salvation. It is an emersion into God's power for service. If salvation were the Holy Spirit baptism, then speaking in tongues should be the outward evidence of folks becoming born again. That would be ludicrous because the outward sign of a person receiving Christ and becoming born again is changed life. It would be wrong to expect folks to speak in tongues to prove their salvation. You cannot add any work to salvation; salvation is by faith alone. If I were to liken you to a glass, and then poured some water in that glass, that water would be the Holy Spirit indwelling you at salvation. If I were to take that same glass, indwelt with some water, and totally submerge it in a bucket filled with water, now you are baptized in the Spirit.

2. **False conclusion #2:** The Holy Spirit baptism is the same as receiving Christ at salvation, but tongues and all miraculous demonstrations of the Holy Spirit have passed away with the first century church (Cessationism). We know this isn't true because Jesus is still doing miracles, signs and wonders through His followers today. People are still being Baptized in the Spirit and receiving a heavenly prayer language.

3. **The truth #1:** There is another experience besides being born again and water baptized. You can be baptized with the Holy Spirit, receive a prayer language, and begin to walk in powerful dimensions of spiritual experience.

4. **The truth #2:** There is one baptism in the Holy Spirit that can be experienced, but many subsequent anointings and fillings. In Acts chapter 2, 120 people were baptized in the Holy Spirit. And then in Acts chapter 4 they were filled with another fresh filling of

the Spirit, which empowered them with boldness (see Acts 4:31). This should encourage you to keep pressing in for fresh fillings and impartations. Listen to what Paul tells the Roman church: *"For I long to see you, that I may impart to you some spiritual gift, so that you may be established." (Romans 1:11)*. There is no end to the blessings and impartations that await the hungry seeker of God. The experience of being baptized in the Holy Spirit is not the end. It's the gateway to richer spiritual experiences.

Hearing and learning all this, and being convinced of the truth, was not enough for me. I wanted to experience it. But how? I shut myself up in my bedroom and asked God to baptize me in the Holy Spirit. Nothing happened. Then I remembered listening to a faith teaching which stated, "you must believe that you receive."

> *Therefore I say to you, whatever things you ask when you pray, believe that you receive them, and you will have them.*
> *~Mark 11:24*

I was convinced that being baptized in the Holy Spirit and receiving a heavenly language was the will of God. The Bible is our final authority for believers and Jesus commanded His disciples to be filled with the power of the Holy Spirit (see Luke 24:49 and Acts 1:4-8). If this is the will of God and it's all over in the Bible, what was I afraid of? Then I read these passages in the Gospel of Luke:

> *If a son asks for bread from any father among you, will he give him a stone? Or if he asks for a fish, will he give him a serpent instead of a fish? Or if he asks for an egg, will he offer him a scorpion? If you then, being evil, know how to give good gifts to your children, how much more will your heavenly Father give the Holy Spirit to those who ask Him!   ~Luke 11:11-13*

SPIRIT WORLD

I was convinced that God wasn't going to give me a demon or a snake if I asked for the Holy Spirit. Then the thought occurred to me that when I asked for the Holy Spirit baptism, I should believe that I receive it. If I have truly received it by faith when I ask, then I should just start speaking in tongues…so I started making up syllables. It sounded like gibberish but there was no one there to mock me so I kept right on making up a language. I remember as a kid riding in the car with my Dad and he would sometimes listen to a festive sounding Mexican radio show where the announcer would motor on in Spanish. Once in a while I would understand a word or two. As children, we would mimic the language from the back seat. It was nothing for us to mimic the sounds of German, French or Spanish. So it was not difficult for me to make up something that sounded like a real language.

This went on for only a couple of minutes where I was making up a language when suddenly… the presence of the Holy Spirit flooded my bedroom. My emotions were going haywire and I was seized by God's loving, holy power. Out of my spirit came an articulate language and I knew I was not making it up anymore. The heavenly language just poured out of my mouth and I was enraptured in that state for ten or fifteen minutes, just worshiping and praying in my new language. Since that day I have never stopped using my prayer language. I pray in tongues when I drive my car. I pray in tongues when I'm doing mundane chores. I pray in tongues every day. These words in John's gospel came to mind:

> *"He who believes in Me, as the Scripture has said, out of his heart will flow rivers of living water." But this He spoke concerning the Spirit, whom those believing in Him would receive; for the Holy Spirit was not yet given, because Jesus was not yet glorified.* ~John 7:38-39

Why do They Speak in Tongues?

I met a guy who told me that he had once been baptized in the Holy Spirit and used to pray in tongues all the time. Once, while he was driving his car and praying in tongues, he heard a voice tell him to stop praying in tongues and never do it again. He believed it was God who told him to stop praying in tongues, so he never prayed in tongues again. I told him, "The voice you heard couldn't have been God because God never speaks contrary to His word. The Bible says, *"Therefore, brethren, desire earnestly to prophesy, and do not forbid to speak with tongues" (1 Corinthians 14:39)*. God's word says not to forbid speaking in tongues, so it wasn't Him who told you to stop speaking in tongues."

He wasn't convinced, so I asked him to tell me about his life since he stopped praying in tongues. He told me that since he had stopped praying in tongues at least fifteen years earlier, he had two failed marriages and he struggles with addictions. He hadn't been able to hold a job for more than two years and he had hopped around from church, to church, to church. I tried to explain to him that there were two reasons I believed he heard from the devil and not from God:

1. The voice he heard was contrary to the Bible.
2. He had NOT experienced a victorious life since he listened to that voice.

I prayed with him and he sensed a real peace from God. He expressed that he wasn't ready to pray in tongues again yet, but I gave him a lot to think on. I encouraged him to go to a Spirit-filled church where tongues and the gifts of the Spirit are practiced. I have this theory that if you walk along a slippery creek bank long enough, sooner or later you'll slip in. You will become what you associate with. If you hang around Spirit-filled believers long enough, sooner or later you'll get filled with the Holy Spirit.

GIVING MESSAGES IN TONGUES

After I gave my life to Christ, I was invited to a young men's discipleship class, which was a very intense bible study. We met in our Pastor's living room. The attendance varied, it would range anywhere from six to fifteen men per class. The meetings started with everyone standing up and praying in the Spirit (tongues) for ten to fifteen minutes. Sometimes we would also sing in the Spirit. We prayed until a unified pause would settle over the group. Everyone just knew that we were done because the peace of God would settle over us and we had a sense that many things had been prayed through. When peace would settle over us, we would wait on God while absorbing the atmosphere.

At one of those meetings, as we waited on God, I had this burden to speak out loud in tongues. It was a very strong impression and I didn't know what to do with it. I had never prophesied before or given any kind of Holy Spirit utterance. I held back, not knowing what to do to the point where I almost felt ashamed and compelled to give it. I am reminded of a couple of scripture verses about this:

> *I was mute with silence,*
> *I held my peace even from good;*
> *And my sorrow was stirred up.*
> *My heart was hot within me;*
> *While I was musing, the fire burned.*
> *Then I spoke with my tongue.* ~Psalm 39:2-3

> *Then I said, "I will not make mention of Him,*
> *Nor speak anymore in His name."*
> *But His word was in my heart like a burning fire*
> *Shut up in my bones;*
> *I was weary of holding it back,*
> *And I could not.* ~Jeremiah 20:9

Why do They Speak in Tongues?

Finally, the pastor said, "Someone has a word or a tongue from God. Just go ahead and be obedient. Move out in faith and give that word." How did he know what God was doing inside me? He was very sensitive to the Holy Spirit. I launched out by faith and spoke a message in tongues that was to be interpreted. This tongue did not sound like my prayer language. It sounded reminiscent of French. The pastor had studied different dialects of French in graduate school and could understand most of what I was saying. I have never had a lesson in French my whole life. Although he could have translated the message, he chose to wait on the Lord for one of the guys to interpret it by the Spirit. A young man spoke out the interpretation with the familiar phrase, *"Thus says the Lord..."* My Pastor listened intently on the interpretation that came forth and explained that he understood the language and that the interpretation given was right on. An interpretation is not a word-for-word translation, but it gives the gist of the message.

At another discipleship meeting, I again gave a message in tongues. This time the tongue sounded like German. There was a guy at the meeting who studied German in college and could have translated much of the word given, but followed the example of the Pastor and waited on God for someone else to give the interpretation. The interpretation came forth and was right on. You have to understand, both the person who gave the message in tongues and the person who interpreted it did not know the language spoken. The person gave the interpretation completely by the Holy Spirit. My friend who understood German said the tongue was a high German and explained some of the words and their meaning. We were completely blown away.

> *Though I speak with the tongues of men and of angels, but have not love, I have become sounding brass or a clanging cymbal.*   ~1 Corinthians 13:1

SPIRIT WORLD

Notice that in this verse there are languages of men; French, German and so on, and there are angelic languages. According to infoplease.com, there are roughly 6,500 spoken languages today. This does not account for extinct languages. When someone is baptized in the Holy Spirit, and receives a prayer language, it could be an earthly tongue, a heavenly tongue, or an extinct language.

I know some people from South Africa who have told me of a tribe of Bushmen that speak in clicking sounds. That's right, clicking sounds. The languages on earth are so many and diverse. Never assume that the supernatural tongue someone is speaking isn't a real language.

> *But the manifestation of the Spirit is given to each one for the profit of all: for to one is given the word of wisdom through the Spirit, to another the word of knowledge through the same Spirit, to another faith by the same Spirit, to another gifts of healings by the same Spirit, to another the working of miracles, to another prophecy, to another discerning of spirits, to another different kinds of tongues, to another the interpretation of tongues. But one and the same Spirit works all these things, distributing to each one individually as He wills.*   ~1 Corinthians 12:7-11

Notice that when these verses speak of spiritual gifts given to the church, they state that some have the ability to speak in different kinds of tongues. Some people can speak in many different languages by the Holy Spirit. When I pray to God in tongues, my prayer language sounds pretty much the same. When I have given messages in tongues that need to be interpreted, I've spoken in several different languages. There have been times when I entered into deep intercession and my prayer language changed to a different language. I don't have to be a linguist to hear that the sounds and intonation of my normal prayer language have changed into something totally different.

You will notice that the grace gifts of the Holy Spirit fall naturally into three different categories:

1. **The Vocal Gifts:** Prophecy, tongues, and interpretation of tongues.
2. **The Discernment Gifts:** Words of wisdom, words of knowledge, and discerning of spirits.
3. **The Power Gifts:** Faith, working of miracles, and gifts of healing.

The Holy Spirit wants to manifest Himself through our lives in many diverse and dynamic ways. The Baptism in the Holy Spirit is the gateway to the supernatural. When you receive this baptism, you are receiving power to be a greater witness. Being a witness means that you give evidence to the risen Lord. You become a proof producer in the court of public opinion. Christians were always meant to walk in the power of God. You need the power of God to live victoriously in front of the world. Your witness is demonstrated through word, deed, and lifestyle.

If you were to give testimony in a court of law, the opposing attorney would try to discredit your witness by pointing to your surly lifestyle. Your lifestyle matters and you need the power of the Holy Spirit to overcome destructive habits and addictions. Your character matters. The world is watching. What speaks to them is that you are learning to overcome by your walk with God. The bottom line to the world is: "Does this Jesus stuff help me survive and thrive in life?" When you receive the Baptism in the Holy Spirit, your life will scream out YES!

I share with you in the next chapter how being baptized in the Holy Spirit, and praying in tongues, has radically transformed my personal prayer life for the good.

When we pray in tongues, the Bible says that we are praying divine secrets; mysteries. The Holy Spirit understands and is also prompting and praying through you.

SPIRIT WORLD

Chapter 10

WHY DO I SPEAK IN TONGUES?

Now it came to pass, as He was praying in a certain place, when He ceased, that one of His disciples said to Him, "Lord, teach us to pray, as John also taught his disciples."
So He said to them, "When you pray, say:
Our Father in heaven,
Hallowed be Your name.
Your kingdom come.
Your will be done.
On earth as it is in heaven.
Give us day by day our daily bread.
And forgive us our sins,
For we also forgive everyone who is indebted to us.
And do not lead us into temptation,
But deliver us from the evil one." ~Luke 11:1-4 NKJV

The above prayer is commonly known as the "Our Father" prayer. I was raised in a traditional church and had memorized this amazing prayer at a young age. I didn't really know how to pray to an invisible God, so once in a while I would pray the "Our Father" prayer. I figured it pretty much covered everything, although not the specifics, so why should I pray any more. The prayer covers worship, forgiveness, petitioning for my needs, and protection from evil. You could say that my prayer and worship life were pretty surface, to say the least. However, after I received the baptism in the Holy Spirit my prayer life was catapulted into a whole new level.

Because I was truly born again and then baptized in the Holy Spirit, my spiritual senses became highly tuned. I would get prayer burdens and had to pray in tongues. Sometimes I was praying for an individual, and sometimes there was something happening in the spiritual atmosphere at my work. Sometimes I was praying for my life to stay in the will of God. I would almost always have a sense of what I was praying for, but not the specifics. Then when I switched over to praying in English, I found I could articulate things and enter a flow. The rich depth that receiving a prayer language has added to my prayer life cannot be understated.

PRAYING THROUGH TO PEACE

Be anxious for nothing, but in everything by prayer and supplication, with thanksgiving, let your requests be made known to God; and the peace of God, which surpasses all understanding, will guard your hearts and minds through Christ Jesus. ~Philippians 4:6-7

Many times, a quick, genuflect prayer does not lift the burden and give you peace. Some things require you to pray through to peace. Having the ability to pray in tongues will help you tremendously. Often the prayer burden I receive comes in the form of anxiety. Not a panic, but an anxious burden with a sense of urgency. I have noticed that it usually takes me 20 to 45 minutes of praying in the spirit for a burden to lift. There are times when it takes much longer. There are times I have

SPIRIT WORLD

prayed through to peace, but in my spirit I knew that this prayer burden was not over. It was going to require me to go back at it for many days until the war was won. At times, you can win battles and skirmishes, but still not win the war. These nuances and types of prayer burdens are only known to veteran intercessors.

Many Christians are robbed of a victorious prayer life because they never pray through to victory and peace. There are some things you can ask for one time and it is done. There are other things that take a concerted prayer effort. I can't always give explanations as to why some things are harder to pray through to victory than others, they just are. Praying in tongues can help you to pray for things that your mind cannot comprehend.

I recall a National Day of Prayer in 2001. I was a youth pastor at a small church in Alma, Michigan, and the position could only pay a part-time salary. I loved the work, but knew that I had to get another job to supplement my income. It was a low time in my life; I was 40 years old and had a Master's degree in theology, and still I was not yet in full-time ministry. Needless to say, I had some things to pray through.

The National Day of Prayer is an annual observance on the first Thursday of May. It was created by a joint resolution of the United States Congress, and signed into law by President Harry S. Truman in 1952. It invites people of all faiths to pray for our nation. There are prayer breakfasts which include pomp and circumstance political gatherings where high profile religious leaders and local politicians pray and bloviate. Although many of these event aspects are good, I have yet to see many designated prayer meetings. Instead of feasting, playing and politicking, how about some fasting and praying? Unity is good, sustained unified prayer is better.

Why do I Speak in Tongues?

I decided to skip the local prayer breakfast and fast and pray in the church sanctuary. I arrived at 8:30 a.m. and was determined to pray and worship until God spoke to me. I needed some assurance of His call on my life. I needed to know I was in the will of God. I needed a JOB! So I turned on the worship music at a low volume and started pacing while praying in tongues.

Periodically, people came into the sanctuary, prayed for a bit and then left. I would acknowledge them but continued my prayer vigil. Three hours had passed without me really noticing. I worshiped while singing and praying in tongues. Sometimes I would look up a Bible verse, but mostly I just paced while praying in tongues. Finally I felt the atmosphere change. I felt faith rise in my heart and the thick presence of the Holy Spirit descended into the sanctuary. It was in this atmosphere of heaven that I went into a vision.

In the vision, I saw a tall rocky mountain. There was a path that was angling and twisting toward the top of the mountain. Christians and truth seekers were on a pilgrimage to the top of the mountain. Parts of the trail were dangerous, dark and hard to navigate. At one narrow dark section of the path that was close to the top, I was standing on a rock face overlooking the pilgrims ascending the trail. As I shouted encouragement to them, a magnificent angel stood behind and above me. He was tall with thick flowing blond hair. He glowed a brilliant light that partly illuminated the trail. Then he raised a huge, double edged sword. As the sword was extended out in front of him, held with two mighty fists and pointing upwards, it began to glow and glisten. The sword became brighter and brighter until a magnificent light emanated over the dark side of the mountain. The light gave more than illumination to the travelers, it also gave hope, strength, faith, and encouragement to them.

SPIRIT WORLD

The interpretation came very easily. The encouragement of the Holy Spirit swept all over me as the vision reinforced my calling to teach and encourage the body of Christ with the illuminated sword of the Spirit, which is the word of God. As I am faithful to teach and to preach, God's angel will shine the sword of the Spirit. The Word of God is a double-edged sword, both New and Old Testament. The saints and pilgrims walking the narrow path need the flaming light of God's Word to give them strength and illumination in a dark world.

> *Your word is a lamp to my feet*
> *And a light to my path.* ~Psalm 119:105

> *For the word of God is living and powerful, and sharper than any two-edged sword, piercing even to the division of soul and spirit, and of joints and marrow, and is a discerner of the thoughts and intents of the heart.* ~Hebrews 4:13

This is an example of how we can pray through to peace and victory. It was only a few months after my prayer and vision experience that I was in full-time ministry and Pastoring my first church. By praying in the Holy Spirit, a path was blazed for God to take me and my ministry to the next level. Don't ever despise praying through in tongues. What victories await those who will use the spiritual weapons at hand! If you are feeling trapped and falling short of your heavenly calling, do some work in the spiritual realm. Pray in tongues until the assurance comes. If you want the battle to go nuclear, fast (go without food) and pray in the Holy Spirit.

PRAYING DIVINE SECRETS AND THE PREFECT WILL OF GOD

Pursue love, and desire spiritual gifts, but especially that you may prophesy. For he who speaks in a tongue does not speak

> *to men but to God, for no one understands him; however, in the spirit he speaks mysteries.* ~*1 Corinthians 14:1-2*

Pursue love and desire spiritual gifts. This is the perfect balance between having the character of Christ (love), and the power of Christ (spiritual gifts). Just being a loving, nice guy, with no power to set anyone free is no good. Being super spiritual and prophetic but having no character and self-discipline will bring shame. We need both, the fruit of the Spirit (see Galatians 5:22-23) and the powerful gifts of the Spirit (see 1 Corinthians 12:7-11), including praying in tongues.

When we pray in tongues, the Bible says that we are praying divine secrets; mysteries. It's not to men, or for the benefit of the people around you, to understand what you are praying. You are praying directly to God in code. The Holy Spirit understands and is also prompting and praying through you. When you give a message in tongues, it is also to be interpreted. But when you are praying to God in tongues, you are praying divine secrets.

One time I heard a man say that he didn't need to EVER pray in tongues because he could pray everything that needed to be prayed in English (his vernacular language). That all sounds noble on the surface, but if you stop to think about it, it smacks of pride. How can I always be able to formulate and articulate the perfect will of God with my limited language and inadequate understanding? If the Holy Spirit wants to pray through me but I can only pray in my native language, He is limited because I am limited.

If I give myself to praying in the Holy Spirit (tongues), the Spirit can go beyond the limitations of my language and imagination.

> *Now to Him who is able to do exceedingly abundantly above all that we ask or think, according to the power that works in us,*

to Him be glory in the church by Christ Jesus to all generations, forever and ever. Amen. ~Ephesians 3:20-21

TRAVAIL IN THE SPIRIT

Likewise the Spirit also helps in our weaknesses. For we do not know what we should pray for as we ought, *but the Spirit Himself makes intercession for us* **with groanings which cannot be uttered.** *Now He who searches the hearts knows what the mind of the Spirit is, because* **He makes intercession for the saints according to the will of God.** ~Romans 8:26-27

The Holy Spirit helps us in our weakness and limitations. He makes intercessions according to the will of God! There is also a prayer that goes beyond tongues. The Holy Spirit can pray though His saints with groanings which cannot be uttered. It's a deep, inward travail that cannot be articulated into any form of speech or language.

- The New Living Translation states Romans 8:26 this way: *"But the Holy Spirit prays for us with groanings that cannot be expressed in words."*

- The Amplified Bible states Romans 8:26 this way: *"…but the Spirit Himself goes to meet our supplication and pleads on our behalf with unspeakable yearnings and groanings too deep for utterance."*

At different prayer meetings over the years, I have heard some intercessors actually groan, or travail in the spirit. If you think tongues is a little "out there," then this might really be out of your wheel house. This is a book about spiritual experiences so I am not holding anything back. The Bible says to test all things; hold fast what is good (see 1 Thessalonians 5:21). How do we test spiritual experience? We measure it with the Word of God and we look at its fruitfulness. By judging its fruitfulness, I mean we look to see what it produces. The Bible is the ultimate judge, NOT my personal comfort zone. People are often uncomfortable with something new, or that they don't understand, so they have a knee jerk reaction and immediately try to quench the Spirit. Just because we haven't experienced something doesn't mean it isn't legit.

I'm going to make a case for this experience. First, let's see if it's in the Word of God, and then let's look at some of my experiences with groaning in the Spirit, or as some refer to it, travail.

- Jesus groaned within Himself just before He raised Lazarus from the dead. For the Bible to record that He groaned in an intercession before one of His greatest miracles, it must have been heard. *"Therefore, when Jesus saw her weeping, and the Jews who came with her weeping, **He groaned in the spirit and was troubled**" (John 11:33)*.

- Paul said that we as Christians groan inwardly because we desire to be in our eternal resurrected body (see Romans 8:23 and 2 Corinthians 5:2-4). We are in travail for the completion of our salvation.

- Paul said that all of creation groans for the curse to be lifted, and for the manifestation of the sons of light (see Romans 8:22).

- Paul said that he labored in travail (birth pangs, or groaning in the spirit) until Christ was formed in the Galatian Christians (see Galatians 4:19).

Before she was in labor, she gave birth;
Before her pain came,
She delivered a male child.
Who has heard such a thing?
Who has seen such things?

SPIRIT WORLD

Shall the earth be made to give birth in one day?
Or shall a nation be born at once?
For as soon as Zion was in labor,
She gave birth to her children.   ~Isaiah 66:7-8

I was serving at a church in Saginaw, Michigan in the 1990's as the chaplain for the Christian school and the Youth Pastor. One of my functions as the school chaplain was to secure special speakers for the chapel service once a week. I had scheduled someone I believed to be a really cool evangelist. He had been a college star athlete and was an easy 9 or 10 on the coolness meter. The worship that chapel morning was amazing. Many of the children came forward during the worship and were praising God very deeply and sincerely.

Then, as we were winding the worship down and preparing to make that transition from worship service to the invitation of our special speaker, about a dozen children were weeping and travailing in intercession. They were all up in front of the worship team. Their ages ranged from 6 and 7, to 12 or 13 years old. Some were on their knees, rocking back and forth, weeping and groaning. I didn't know what to do. I had never experienced anything like this before. For young children to spontaneously break out into deep intercession was completely foreign to me. I considered stopping them as gently as possible. After all, I had a cool special speaker and I had no idea what he was thinking about all of this. As I stood there, wading through my indecisiveness, our guest speaker grabbed the microphone and said, "Don't stop these kids from praying! If they stop, I will stop and go home! They are birthing something by the Holy Spirit!"

The church had been praying about hosting revival meetings for several months. Several of us from the church had visited the Toronto Blessing (a famous revival that broke out at the Toronto Airport Church in Toronto, Canada in 1994), and we wanted some itinerate evangelists from the revival to come. A short time after these children were travailing in the spirit, we had a minister come from the Toronto Blessing and we had explosive results. We experienced a revival at that church. The football field served as our overflow parking lot and was packed with cars. Inside the church it was standing room only. Many people were refreshed, healed, delivered and saved. We began hosting these meetings once a month for a couple of years. I certainly connected the dots between the children interceding with travail and the outpouring of the Holy Spirit that followed. The Holy Spirit can birth some amazing things through us in prayer. *"For as soon as Zion was in labor, she gave birth to her children" (Isaiah 66:8).*

When I was dating my wife to be, Nicole, I was sometimes confused as to whether or not I should propose marriage. To this day I cannot accurately explain why I was struggling with the thought of marriage. It wasn't because I didn't love her; when we were apart my desire was to be with her. For all intents and purposes, she seemed to be the perfect fit. We conversed well together, we both loved the Lord and felt a call to ministry, we were both musicians, and as an extra bonus she was really hot and made my blood boil.

There was a spiritual war going on inside me. You could try to analyze it and categorize it as a fear of commitment and responsibility, or fear of failure, but it was a spiritual battle. The enemy of our souls fights our forward progression. Anything that is God's best is the enemies worst. His modus operandi is to steal, kill and destroy. His thievery is not limited to what you already possess; he also will try to keep you from future blessings by stealing God opportunities from you.

I was going through one of my spiritual battles and told Nicole that we should take a little break from one another. Nicole had reached a point of total exasperation with me and was on the edge of telling me just what I should do with my little dating break. She began praying about whether she should call it quits on our relationship.

During that time, Nicole and I had mutual friends and a family invited her over for a prayer meeting. Unbeknownst to her, they also invited me to the prayer meeting. I pulled into the driveway and Nicole thought, "Oh no, what is HE doing here?" Another person the family invited was a locally renowned intercessor. She was like Anna in the Gospel of Luke. Anna was a prophetess and a widow who did not depart from the Temple, but served God with fasting and prayers night and day (see Luke 2:36-38). The Anna of the Bible is an example of a true intercessor's call. Remarkably, this invited woman was also an older single woman and her name was Ann. When there was a prayer meeting, Ann was there. She had also been known to go into travail from time to time. This caused consternation for most Pastors who didn't know how to deal with the weirdness of someone descending into a shrill moan at an otherwise tame prayer meeting with dignitaries.

We gathered and began praying for one another. It started out as a normal Pentecostal prayer meeting (if you can call any Pentecostal prayer meeting normal). When they got to me, they gathered around me, laid hands on me, and began praying in tongues. Then things began to get unusual. As Ann prayed she suddenly entered into a spiritual travail. It made the hair on the back of my neck stand up. I started to cringe and wanted her to stop. Although outwardly my flesh was repelling her caterwauling, I had a spiritual sense that something was being broken over me. Her wailing would come in short waves and every time she started to travail, I would weep. When she stopped, I stopped weeping. This happened three or four times and then I felt something leave me. Some oppression had lifted and the heavens were opened.

God spoke clearly to me in an inner audible voice. "Nicole is the one I have chosen for you. Marry her. If you do not marry her, you will not fulfill everything I have called you to do. Choose this day a blessing or curse." At that moment, all fear and vacillation about marrying Nicole had vanished. There was no more double mindedness. I set my face like flint and did not doubt our calling to be together.

Not every person that is faced with the decision to marry has to have this type of experience, or confirmation. For most, a strong witness in their heart is sufficient. Also, travail, or groaning in the Spirit, is not common. I haven't seen this practiced often. My point in sharing this section about travail is to expose you, the reader, to spiritual experience. True spiritual experience should be organic and not manufactured. If it is truly a manifestation of the Holy Spirit and not a performance by someone trying to be super spiritual, it will bear good fruit. In my case, it set me free.

MORE REASONS TO PRAY IN TONGUES

- **The tongue is the rudder of your soul.** When you pray in tongues, you are steering your life into the will of God. *"Indeed, we put bits in horses' mouths that they may obey us, and we turn their whole body. Look also at ships: although they are so large and are driven by fierce winds, they are turned by a very small rudder wherever the pilot desires. Even so the tongue is a little member and boasts great things" (James 3:3-5).*

- **When you pray in tongues you are edifying yourselves.** The word "edify" comes from the word "edifice," which is a tall building. To edify is to build up. When I pray in tongues I am building a greater capacity in my spirit for more revelation of God. *"He who speaks in a tongue edifies himself, but he who prophesies edifies the church" (1 Corinthians 14:4).*

- **When you pray in tongues you are refreshing your inner man.** *"For with stammering lips and another tongue He will speak to this people, to whom He said, 'This is the rest with which You may cause the weary to rest,' and, 'This is the refreshing'; yet they would not hear" (Isaiah 28:11-12).*

- **When you pray in tongues you are building up your faith.** *"But you, beloved, building yourselves up on your most holy faith, praying in the Holy Spirit" (Jude 20).*

- **When you pray in tongues you are entering another dimension of worship.** Prayer is not just petition. It is all forms of communication with God. The highest form of prayer is praising and worshiping Him. In Acts 2:11, the 120 people were speaking in tongues and magnifying God. Worshiping and singing in tongues are a form of prophetic praise. *"What is the conclusion then? I will pray with the spirit, and I will also pray with the understanding. I will sing with the spirit, and I will also sing with the understanding" (1 Corinthians 14:15).*

Conclusion

There are times I get an overwhelming prayer burden. I will attempt to explain what a prayer burden is like. Sometimes, it comes in the form of anxiety. Not an anxiety attack, but an inner anxiousness that I discern as a prayer burden. When I get that spiritual feeling, I am drawn to pray in the Holy Spirit. The Holy Spirit knows what is going on. My mind may not be able to comprehend what the burden is about, but I trust the Holy Spirit. Most of the time the Holy Spirit impresses on me what I'm praying about, albeit in a general sense. For example, I get a sense that I am praying for my children, or family, or I may get a sense that I am praying for my day and God is protecting me from something. At times

Why do I Speak in Tongues?

I have gotten a sense that a spiritual attack has been mounted against me, and by prayer in the Holy Spirit it is being countered.

There are times I have faith lapse anxieties. I doubt whether I am in the will of God in my life pursuits. I may be struggling with a great challenge that has me doubting the outcome, etcetera. In those situations of doubt, I pray in my heavenly language. I pray in tongues until I feel a release and a peace. Like I stated earlier in this chapter, it takes me an average of 20 to 45 minutes of praying in tongues to shake spiritual pressure. God is true to His word. He said that if we pray in the Holy Spirit we will build up our most holy faith.

> *But you, beloved, building yourselves up on your most holy faith, praying in the Holy Spirit.* ~Jude 20

I challenge people to pray in their heavenly language for 20 to 45 minutes straight and see what happens. You cannot walk away from praying in tongues for that short period of time and not sense a lift in your spirit. Your faith is activated to fresh heights and worry dissipates. Praying in tongues for a period of time causes you to enter a rest and a refreshing. If you have not been baptized in the Holy Spirit, with the initial physical evidence of speaking in tongues, why put it off a day longer?

> *If a son asks for bread from any father among you, will he give him a stone? Or if he asks for a fish, will he give him a serpent instead of a fish? Or if he asks for an egg, will he offer him a scorpion? If you then, being evil, know how to give good gifts to your children,* **how much more will your heavenly Father give the Holy Spirit to those who ask Him!** ~Luke 11:11-13

Our God is a good Father and wants you to have the fullness of the Holy Spirit. All you have to do is ask! John the Baptist said that Jesus would be your baptizer in the Holy Spirit.

Why do I Speak in Tongues?

I indeed baptize you with water unto repentance, but He who is coming after me is mightier than I, whose sandals I am not worthy to carry. He will baptize you with the Holy Spirit and fire. ~Matthew 3:11

Repeat the following prayer and then step out in faith by beginning to speak in a heavenly language. Out of your belly will come a river of life; a wellspring of refreshing, and a fountain of joy. You will be able to dip into this cool, fresh spring any time you want. Paul said, *"I will pray with the spirit, and I will also pray with the understanding"* (see 1 Corinthians 14:15). He prayed at will, and you will be able to pray in tongues any time you want.

Dear Lord Jesus,
I recognize that you are the baptizer in the Holy Spirit and fire. I need fresh fire and inner strength to run the race with patience. I ask right now that you would fill me with Your Holy Spirit now. By faith I will begin to speak in tongues as the spirit is enabling me. Thank you, God, for your goodness.
In Jesus' name, Amen

Now, step out in faith and let a heavenly language pour out of you!

*Pursue love, and desire spiritual gifts,
but especially that you may prophecy.*
1 Corinthians 14:1

Chapter 11

DESIRE TO PROPHESY

*Pursue love, and **desire spiritual gifts**, but especially that you may prophesy.*   ~1 Corinthians 14:1

Here the Bible is very clear that we should desire spiritual gifts and ESPECIALLY that we should prophecy. The apostle is referring to the spiritual gifts of the Holy Spirit described in 1 Corinthians 12:7-11. There are nine gifts: three for **seeing**, three for **speaking**, and three for **doing**. The three discernment gifts, or **seeing gifts** are: discerning of spirits, word of wisdom, and the word of knowledge. The three **doing gifts** are: working of miracles, a gift of faith, and gifts of healing. The three **speaking gifts** are: speaking in different kinds of tongues, interpretation of tongues, and prophecy. When I refer to "prophetic gifts" I'm referring mostly to the seeing and speaking gifts.

The word for "desire" in the Greek is: zeloo, (Strong's #2206): To be zealous, to burn with desire, to pursue ardently, to desire earnestly or intensely. This is the kind of desire I have for my first cup of coffee in the morning. I should also burn for the prophetic gifts to awaken in my life. According to 1 Corinthians 12:7-11, the prophetic giftings are very important to victorious living. We need to ardently pursue to move in these giftings. This admonition is not just given to some fringe Pentecostal Churches; this is given to every Christian.

Do we see this kind of pursuit for the prophetic to awaken in our churches and personal lives? From my perspective, I have seen the complete opposite. The cultivation of the gifts of the Holy Spirit described in 1 Corinthians 12:7-11 are not taking place. I believe there are several reasons why prophecy and spiritual gifts are being quenched, such as:

1. In some cases, the leadership doesn't know how to give a prophecy or a Word of Knowledge. It's difficult to lead people into something that you yourself have never experienced. In some Charismatic/Pentecostal circles, the prophetic has been so quenched that a new generation of leaders are being raised up who know nothing of the spiritual gifts.

2. The leadership is afraid of appearing weird and acting weird. First of all, we should be confident as leaders to be able to give explanation and keep things balanced. There is always a risk that even after biblical explanation some will think it's a bit weird. I believe in trying our best to be seeker friendly, but not to the extent where we quench the Holy Spirit. We all want to grow our churches, but let's face it, not everyone visiting your church wants the fullness of the Spirit. Some just want a safe little "God fix" to sooth their conscience and to make sure their eternal life insurance is paid up. Personally, I think people need the "shock and awe" of the prophetic gifts displayed in our services. The worst thing that can happen is that people visit our churches and leave indifferent.

The secrets of their hearts should be revealed and they should fall on their faces, worship God and report that God is truly among them (see 1 Corinthians 14:24-25).

3. Abuse of the prophetic gifts may have taken place and this causes the leadership to be turned off to the spiritual gifts. Have seen it. Experienced it. Bought the t-shirt. I went through a time as a senior pastor when I shut down the prophetic. I was so disgusted with the manipulation that was happening. After a time, while I was reading my Bible one morning, going through my bible-through-the-year program, I read 1 Corinthians 14:1, *"Pursue love, and desire spiritual gifts, but especially that you may prophecy."* The Lord spoke to me so clearly in my spirit, "Why have you stopped the prophetic in my church? It's time to nurture it again." I had to establish some guidelines of prophetic etiquette; simple ground rules for who, how, and when the prophetic gifts would be used in the church. It's a labor of love to train and correct people as they learn to move in the prophetic. And yet, that is what leadership is supposed to do, to raise up people in the things of the Spirit and the fullness of the Word of God. Later in this chapter I discuss prophetic etiquette and pastoring a prophetic people.

PROPHECY IS FOR YOUR ENCOURAGEMENT

But he who prophesies speaks edification and exhortation and comfort to men. ~1 Corinthians 14:3

The general disposition of prophecy is to comfort you, build you up, and encourage you. I could go on and on about all the times a prophetic word came at just the right time to bring great encouragement to me.

SPIRIT WORLD

There was a time I worked in sales, and after a year of hard work I was not seeing a financial breakthrough. In many types of sales work, you must build a clientele base before you can begin to make a good living. I strongly considered quitting; after a year of cold calls and trying to earn repeat business, it just wasn't happening. Discouraged, I went up to the altar at the end of a church service and had one of the elders of the church pray for me. He had a prophetic word for me. He told me that he felt the Lord saying that the harvest was just around the corner. "Don't give up. Persevere." Then he asked if that word bore witness with me? Just as he was speaking the prophecy and asking me what I thought, there was a lift in my spirit. I knew that he was speaking by the Spirit of God. The breakthrough came shortly after that, and I had more customers than I knew what to do with.

The thought occurred to me that I could have quit just before the harvest. If it wasn't for that prophetic word, at the right time, I would have quit. How many times have we plowed the field, removed stones, and planted seed; put blood, sweat and tears into weeding and watering; and then, walked away just before the harvest? There are many times we sow in faith; unlike a garden, we cannot see the work done in the natural. We must have prophetic vision and see through the eyes of faith. The Bible promises a guaranteed harvest for those who persevere.

And let us not grow weary while doing good, for in due season we shall reap if we do not lose heart. ~Galatians 6:9

Those who sow in tears
Shall reap in joy.
He who continually goes forth weeping,
Bearing seed for sowing,
Shall doubtless come again with rejoicing,
Bringing his sheaves with him. ~Psalm 126:5-6

Desire to Prophesy

When I was a young preacher still trying to gain my confidence, I visited a church to hear the guest speaker who had a reputation of being a prophet to the body of Christ. I wasn't sure I had ever seen or heard a prophet before so I was excited to go. The man's name was Dick Mills, who has since passed on and went home to be with Jesus. Dick had an amazing memory of Bible verses and their addresses. When He gave a prophecy to someone, he always had Bible verses to go with it. Without looking in his Bible, he would call out the book, chapter and verse, and then quote it from memory. Sometimes he would quote verses from several different translations, FROM MEMORY. He picked me out of the crowd at this meeting and had me stand up. He prophesied over me that God was going to use my preaching and teaching ministry. (He didn't even know that I was a preacher.) He proclaimed over me that there was healing in my words, and that as I taught the Bible people would be healed in their soul and body. Then he gave me two Bible verses to go with the prophecy:

> *Pleasant words are like a honeycomb,*
> *Sweetness to the soul and health to the bones.*
> ~Proverbs 16:24

> *The Lord GOD has given me*
> *The tongue of the learned,*
> *That I should know how to speak*
> *A word in season to him who is weary.*
> *He awakens me morning by morning,*
> *He awakens my ear*
> *To hear as the learned.*
> ~Isaiah 50:4

To say that this prophetic word from Dick Mills has been an encouragement would be an understatement. I have literally done spiritual warfare with this prophecy. I declare these verses over my sermons. I declare that the words I speak are a word in due season to him who is weary. The Lord will cause healing to all who hear the Word of God that I declare. The Apostle Paul told Timothy to do warfare by the prophecies he had received.

> *This charge I commit to you, son Timothy, according to the prophecies previously made concerning you, that by them you may wage the good warfare.* ~1 Timothy 1:18

How much we need the prophetic in our lives. There are so many times you and I need an encouraging word from God; the right word, at just the right time. When I talk about prophecy being for "encouragement," I am speaking about being **encouraged to do the right thing**. I am not talking about a false encouragement that affirms us even when we are living out of the will of God.

My daughter and I used to watch the reality TV show called American Idol, a singing competition that would award a recording contract to the winner. A sad part of the show was when poor deceived souls who could not sing were contestants. Although they sounded like a cat in a paper sack, in their minds they were going to be the next American Idol. These disillusioned contestants always had an entourage of false prophets and false prophetesses. The fan club was more pathetic than the singer. They were constantly affirming this person that he/she was awesome. Then the moment of truth would come when this "legend in their own mind" would sing before the panel of judges. The true prophetic word would come from the judges, "Don't quit your day job" or, "You need to find another profession for your life, singing is not what you are called to do." WOW! The fecal material really hit the rotary air displacement blade. The terrible singer became highly upset and would cuss out the judges and vow that they would be a star. Then the most amazing thing would happen; the deceived fan club would still be affirming this person that he/she was awesome.

God is not going to set you up for failure. He will encourage you in the right way. Don't be like the deceived American Idol wanna-be; receive correction as well as affirmation. That being said, a prophetic word is not just about pointing out your sin and the worst in your life. It's like digging for gold; when mining, our focus is not on the dirt, but on the golden vein. A prophetic word will sift through the dirt and pull out the golden nuggets of destiny. Anyone can be condemning, but who can see the amazing, divine destiny for your life? Who can see the secret purposes and unrefined abilities in your soul? Only a true prophet of God can encourage you in the way you should take.

HOW TO TEST A PROPHET AND PROPHECIES

Do not quench the Spirit. Do not despise prophecies. Test all things; hold fast what is good.   ~1 Thessalonians 5:19-21

There is so much value and encouragement in the exercise of the prophetic gifts that we should not let the fear of abuse keep us from learning and growing. The Bible is very clear, "Do not quench the Spirit. Do not despise prophecies." But it also admonishes us to "Test all things; hold fast what is good." This is the responsibility of all Christians, but especially the leadership. As shepherds of God's flock, we need to train and guide God's people. This causes me to think of one of the most horrifying words and concepts ever conceived in the Bible; it's called "accountability." There, I said it. In our age of hyper-sensitive, milk-toast, easily offended people, it is a word that causes demons of pride and self-justification to manifest in brilliant Technicolor. But if we are going to nurture the prophetic gifts of the Holy Spirit in our midst, we must have a safe, teachable environment, and a humble, holy people.

The first and best way to test a prophet is to test yourself. Yes, you read it right. If you want to grow in the prophetic you must be teachable and

SPIRIT WORLD

willing to examine yourself. Make sure YOU are ministering out of a pure heart. Before you teach, preach and prophesy to anyone, do a heart check. Do you have an axe to grind? Are you in bitter disagreement with church leadership? Are you angry and bitter? Do you want to let loose and tell folks where to go and what they can do once they get there? Maybe no one has told you this, but it may be a good Idea for you NOT to prophesy when you are angry and bitter.

Moses was told by God to *speak* to a rock and it would yield a river of refreshing water that would quench the thirst of God's people in the dry wilderness (see Numbers 20:7-8). Moses was fed up with the constant whining and complaining of God's people. His stress level had reached the boiling point. Old Mo had a meltdown in front of everyone. Instead of *speaking* to the rock, he *struck it* twice out of anger while yelling "Hear now you rebels! Must we bring water out of this rock?" (see Numbers 20:10).

God became upset with Moses and told him that he failed to hollow, or sanctify Him, in front of the people. And for Moses' display of anger, God forbade him from entering into the Promised Land (see Numbers 20:12). What did God mean when He said that Moses failed to hollow Him in the eyes of Israel? It meant that Moses didn't portray God correctly. God was not angry at that time but Moses portrayed Him as angry. WOW… It's important to God that we portray Him accurately. If we say we are speaking and acting for God, we better make sure our hearts are right. We need to make sure we know His heart on the matter. We must accept the responsibility of speaking for God. If you start to prophesy with "Thus says the Lord" or, "I believe God is saying," make sure the Lord wants it said. Yes, there is grace. Yes, there is room to learn and grow. But if you are a serial abuser of the name of the Lord, you will find yourself in deep trouble with Him.

Desire to Prophesy

You shall not take the name of the LORD your God in vain, for the LORD will not hold him guiltless who takes His name in vain. ~Exodus 20:7

Using the name of the Lord in vain is more than cussing and cursing. It's saying, "God told me" or "God is saying" when He is not saying. This can be dangerous business. First and foremost, make sure your motives are right before you prophesy.

Before we discuss how to test a prophet, we must first see from the Bible that there is a prophetic ministry today. A prophet today is not the same as an Old Testament Prophet. He doesn't carry the same authority. A prophet today is to be judged by the Bible. The Old Testament Prophet *was* the Bible. If you didn't listen to the prophets of old you were to be killed. Also, if the Old Testament Prophets were wrong about a prediction, they were to be killed. The folks got together and had a rock concert, and the false prophet was the star. The prophets today are not writing any more books of the Bible; they encourage us in the already established truth.

The New Testament talks about the prophet's ministry. Prophets are listed in the five-fold ministry (see Ephesians 4:11-12). Also, all believers are encouraged to prophecy (see 1 Corinthians 14:1). All believers can prophesy, but not all believers are called to the ministry gift of a prophet. Someone called to the office of a prophet functions on a higher level and is a leader and equipper. The book of Acts gives testimony to the prophet's ministry continuing on into the New Testament era:

And in these days prophets came from Jerusalem to Antioch. Then one of them, named Agabus, stood up and showed by the Spirit that there was going to be a great famine throughout all the world, which also happened in the days of Claudius Caesar. ~Acts 11:27-28

> *Now Judas and Silas, themselves being prophets also, exhorted and strengthened the brethren with many words.* ~Acts 15:32

We can see that this ministry has not passed away. Some are still called to be prophets. Since this calling is still active, how do we judge the authentic from the false? There are three simple ways to test a prophet and prophecies:

1. We test the **Forthtelling**
2. We test the **Foretelling**
3. We test the **Fruit**

Testing the Forthtelling: Does the prophecy line up with scripture and the character of God as revealed in the Bible?

True New Testament prophets are not adding to the Bible. The Bible is what we (theologians) call a closed canon, or a closed rule of measurement. There were three main tests given to the 27 books of the New Testament.

1. Were they written by an Apostle, or the direct disciple of one? (The Authorship Test)
2. Does the content of the book agree with the rest of Bible? (The Unity Test)
3. Did the early churches receive these writings as authentic and having apostolic authority? (The Witness Test)

When someone preaches, or teaches the Bible, we measure their message by the Bible. The Bible is the final authority for what we believe and how we act. It's the same thing with prophecies. Like preaching, a prophetic word is not equal in authority with the Bible, it's subject to the Bible. We test the authenticity of the message by the Word of God. Unlike the Old Testament writing prophets, we are not writing new books to the Bible; the Bible is a completed book. There are warnings in the Bible about NOT adding or taking away from God's word:

> *For I testify to everyone who hears the words of the prophecy of this book: If anyone adds to these things, God will add to him the plagues that are written in this book; and if anyone takes away from the words of the book of this prophecy, God shall take away his part from the Book of Life, from the holy city, and from the things which are written in this book.*
> ~Revelation 22:18-19

> *You shall not add to the word which I command you, nor take from it, that you may keep the commandments of the LORD your God which I command you.* ~Deuteronomy 4:2

> *Every word of God is pure;*
> *He is a shield to those who put their trust in Him.*
> *Do not add to His words,*
> *Lest He rebuke you, and you be found a liar.* ~Proverbs 30:5-6

If a modern-day prophet comes along and claims that he has a revelation that needs to be added to the Bible, we would reject it. If the prophet claims that his revelation has equal or greater authority than the Bible, we need to reject him as a false prophet. A good example of a false prophet is Joseph Smith, the founder of the Mormon Church. He claimed that the book of Mormon and The Pearl of Great Price are of equal and greater authority than the Bible. Joseph Smith claimed that the Angel Moroni visited him on numerous occasions and one time handed him golden plates with a New Gospel of Jesus Christ. Listen to what the Apostle Paul has to say about Joseph Smith's gospel.

> *I marvel that you are turning away so soon from Him who called you in the grace of Christ, to a different gospel, which is not another; but there are some who trouble you and want to pervert the gospel of Christ. But even if we, or an angel from*

SPIRIT WORLD

heaven, preach any other gospel to you than what we have preached to you, let him be accursed. As we have said before, so now I say again, if anyone preaches any other gospel to you than what you have received, let him be accursed.
~Galatians 1:6-9

Using the forthtelling test on Joseph Smith and the gospel he received from an angel, we can conclude that it is false and not to be received. In the book of Deuteronomy, Moses also gave us the forthtelling test:

If there arises among you a prophet or a dreamer of dreams, and he gives you a sign or a wonder, and the sign or the wonder comes to pass, of which he spoke to you, saying, 'Let us go after other gods' — which you have not known — 'and let us serve them,' you shall not listen to the words of that prophet or that dreamer of dreams, for the LORD your God is testing you to know whether you love the LORD your God with all your heart and with all your soul.   ~Deuteronomy 13:1-3

The Bible tells us about an end time false prophet that will show great signs and wonders but will lead multitudes into deception and the worship of the notorious Antichrist. The only ones who will not be deceived are those who are lovers of truth, and lovers of the true God.

The coming of the lawless one is according to the working of Satan, with all power, signs, and lying wonders, and with all unrighteous deception among those who perish, because they did not receive the love of the truth, that they might be saved!
~2 Thessalonians 2:9-10 (see also Revelation 13:11-18)

As Christians, we must know our Bible and be able to compare prophets and prophecies with the Word of God. All truth is measured by the Word of truth. Start a Bible-through-the-year program. Go to Bible studies at your church. Challenge yourself to know what you believe, and why you believe it.

Desire to Prophesy

But sanctify the Lord God in your hearts, and always be ready to give a defense to everyone who asks you a reason for the hope that is in you, with meekness and fear.   ~1 Peter 3:15

And when they say to you, "Seek those who are mediums and wizards, who whisper and mutter," should not a people seek their God? Should they seek the dead on behalf of the living? To the law and to the testimony! If they do not speak according to this word, it is because there is no light in them.
~Isaiah 8:19-20

As believers in Christ, we don't have to seek false spiritual experiences. We can seek answers from the Word of God. God can send us true prophetic gifts that will strengthen and encourage us in the right way we should take. We can measure prophetic words by the Bible and the witness in our hearts.

Testing the foretelling of prophecy:

But the prophet who presumes to speak a word in My name, which I have not commanded him to speak, or who speaks in the name of other gods, that prophet shall die.' And if you say in your heart, 'How shall we know the word which the LORD has not spoken?' — when a prophet speaks in the name of the LORD, if the thing does not happen or come to pass, that is the thing which the LORD has not spoken; the prophet has spoken it presumptuously; you shall not be afraid of him.
~Deuteronomy 18:20-22

Things were pretty harsh back in those days. If your prophetic word did not come to pass, you were executed. Thank God there is a little more grace today. If you are new in giving prophetic words, try to stay away from predictions. There used to be a saying in Charismatic circles, "No dates, no mates." In other words, never tell people who they should marry, and predicting dates of events is almost always bad. If you feel

SPIRIT WORLD

that God is sharing something with you, write it down in a journal. Pray long and hard about whether you should share it at all. Even though we have the indwelling Holy Spirit today, we still don't always see things clearly. Listen to what Paul says in this verse:

> *For now we see in a mirror, dimly, but then face to face. Now I know in part, but then I shall know just as I also am known.*
> *~1 Corinthians 13:12*

We see through a dim mirror.

I took my wife to a Kim Clement meeting in Detroit Michigan back in the late 1990's. Kim has passed on now, but he was a legitimate prophet of God. His most famous prophecy was the prediction of Donald Trump becoming President of the United States years before the 2016 election. If you listen to any of Kim's prophecies, **they are not always clear.** They are often veiled in symbolism, metaphors, and play-on-word phrases. When he predicted George W. Bush would be president, he said there would be a burning bush in the white house.

Kim Clement's meetings were very radical. He would prophecy with music, sometimes in a rap style. His band would never leave the platform because Kim would start sing preaching his prophetic words and the band would start rocking with him. (You had to be there.)

In one of his meetings that I attended, he announced from the platform that there was someone at the meeting who had a brother that lived in New York City. Two women stood up and he asked them to come up on the platform. He then prophesied that God was doing a great work in their lives. He then asked the women why he was seeing a man in a dress among books. One of the women said that her brother was a homosexual and a librarian. WOW... He asked the other woman to step down and Kim prophesied about the homosexual librarian living in New York. He encouraged the lady still on the platform that her brother would be saved and delivered from the homosexual lifestyle. This is an example of seeing through a dark glass. He was seeing pictures and asked what they meant.

Before the great Pentecostal preacher John Osteen died, he asked Kim Clement to fly to Houston Texas to have lunch with him. John Osteen was the founder and Pastor of Lakewood Church in Houston. During their lunch together, John asked Kim if the illness he was experiencing was going to be terminal. Kim said, "Put your house in order, you are going to die." John then asked Kim who would get his ministry. Kim's response was, "The man who is holding you as you breathe your last breath will receive your mantel and ministry." John's son Joel was holding him as he breathed out his last breath. Joel had never been in the pulpit before his father's death; he edited his father's television broadcasts. While he was editing sermon after sermon, he was hearing his father preaching message after anointed message. When he stepped into the pulpit for the first time, the Elders couldn't believe how much Joel sounded like his father. Joel has gone on to pastor one of the greatest churches in America, his father's Lakewood Church in Houston, Texas.

Although there are true prophets of God whose predictions are amazing, there are also epic blunders. Whenever someone tries to predict the Rapture (see 1 Thessalonians 4:13-18) or the Second Coming of Christ (see Revelation 19), you know it's not going to end well. Listen to these words of Jesus:

> *Watch therefore, for you know neither the day nor the hour in which the Son of Man is coming.* ~Matthew 25:13

Charles Russell, founder of the Watch Tower Society and Tract Society, otherwise known as Jehovah's Witnesses, was most infamous

SPIRIT WORLD

for predicting Christ's Second Coming and being wrong. Almost all of his false predictions for 1878, 1881, 1914, 1918 and 1925 were later reinterpreted as being an invisible coming or initiating some bizarre prophetic event. If someone attempts to predict the Rapture or Second Coming, run away. They are about to make an utter fool of themselves. Or worse, they could go deeper into deception and false doctrine. Charles Russell taught that Jesus was not God, but the first created being, and the Jehovah witnesses still teach this today. The Christian teaching about the incarnation is essential. A mere man could not pay for the sins of the world. God cannot die, so God became man and paid the price for you to be forgiven and have peace with the living God. Only the blood of Jesus, who is "God the Son", can pay for your sins and bring you into a relationship with the living God.

One of the most basic teachings of the Bible and Christianity is that Jesus is God; co-equal with the Father and Holy Spirit. Being a true Christian necessitates that you believe Jesus is God. The doctrine of Christ is called Christology. Jesus existed eternally with God; through Him all things were made; He was born of a virgin; lived a sinless life; died vicariously on the cross for the sins of the world; rose from the grave on the third day; is seated at the right hand of God; He will come again to rule the world; and He is the supreme judge of the living and the dead. Even a cursory reading of the New Testament will reveal Christ as God (see John 1:1-3, 14, John 5:23, 8:24, 58, 10:30-33, Matthew 1:23, Isaiah 9:6, Colossians 1:16). If you don't have the right Jesus, you do not have the right God.

> *Whoever denies the Son does not have the Father either; he who acknowledges the Son has the Father also.* ~1 John 2:23

So, we see that Charles Russell failed two of the tests determining a true prophet. He failed the **Foretelling test** because he made numerous false predictions on an epic scale, and he failed the **Forthtelling test** by teaching heresy.

There are times when a prophecy fails to come to pass and it's not the fault of the prophet. Some prophecies are conditional upon the hearer being obedient. The book of Jonah is a great example; Jonah prophesied to the Ninevites that in forty days Nineveh would be destroyed. Upon hearing the pronounced judgment, the people of Nineveh fasted and repented for their sins. They humbled themselves before God and He relented and did not destroy them. The Prophecy to the Ninevites was conditional upon their repentance and obedience.

Jesus stood on the shore of the sea of Galilee and was being pressed by the crowd that gathered to hear the Word of God. Peter loaned Jesus his fishing boat, and pulling out into the water a short distance from shore, Jesus had a natural amphitheater. No one ever spoke the way that Jesus did, and I'm sure His homily was amazing, but Peter gave no indication that he was impressed. When Jesus finished speaking he repaid Peter for the use of his boat. What was the payment that Jesus gave Peter? It was a prophetic word from God that, if acted on, would bring a great blessing (see Luke 5:1-11). This prophetic word would fall to the ground and mean nothing if it wasn't obeyed.

"Launch out into the deep and let down your nets for a catch." This word from Jesus required action on the part of the hearer. This was a conditional prophecy, and Peter reluctantly submitted to the encouragement of Jesus. This is not the normal way the fishermen fished the Sea of Galilee. They normally fished at night by stretching a net between two boats, and then they put a lantern on both bows so the fish would be attracted to the light and swim into the net. Peter had pointed out that they had toiled all night, nevertheless he decided to do something out of the ordinary. He obeyed the prophetic word and when both boats were filled with

an abundance of fish, Peter fell on his face before Jesus. Notice how the sermon of Jesus didn't impress Peter, but the power of Jesus did.

A prophetic word that bears witness with your spirit could change your life. When I received a prophetic word to persevere in my sales work, I obeyed and reaped a financial harvest.

> *Believe in the LORD your God, and you shall be established; believe His prophets, and you shall prosper.*
> *~2 Chronicles 20:20b*

If a prophet has a proven track record, and is generally approved by the body of Christ, you need to give his prophetic words serious consideration.

Testing the fruitfulness of prophecy:

> *Beware of false prophets, who come to you in sheep's clothing, but inwardly they are ravenous wolves. You will know them by their fruits. Do men gather grapes from thorn bushes or figs from thistles? Even so, every good tree bears good fruit, but a bad tree bears bad fruit. A good tree cannot bear bad fruit, nor can a bad tree bear good fruit. Every tree that does not bear good fruit is cut down and thrown into the fire. Therefore by their fruits you will know them.* ~Matthew 7:15-20

When you look at the fruit of something, you are looking at what it produces. We already looked at the prophetic words themselves: What is the forthtelling? Do they prophesy according to God's Word? What is the foretelling? Do the prophetic words they give come to pass? These things are outward fruit for sure, but now let's look at the character of the prophet himself, or herself, whatever the case may be.

As teachers, preachers and prophets to the body of Christ, we impart more than just our words and teachings, we impart who we are. We impart ourselves. If we are arrogant, our teaching and preaching will be laced with arrogance. Along with what might be the rightly divided Word of God, arrogance will be infused into the hearers. If the teacher has a self-righteous, legalistic, religious spirit, that will be evidenced in his teachings. If the teacher is rebellious, sneaky and isolates himself, that spirit will be laced into his teachings. I think you get my point. This is because we don't just teach what we know, we impart who we are. The worst cocktail that can be served to Christians is arrogance mixed with ignorance. The next mixed drink from hell is a rebellious Margarita with a lemon twist of stubbornness.

> *For rebellion is as the sin of witchcraft,*
> *And stubbornness is as iniquity and idolatry.* ~1 Samuel 15:23a

The Apostle John addressed the rebellious conduct of a church leader in one of his letters. It wasn't the teaching, but the character and actions of the leader that he was correcting. What kind of fruit is produced by the prophet?

> *I wrote to the church, but Diotrephes, who loves to have the preeminence among them, does not receive us. Therefore, if I come, I will call to mind his deeds which he does, prating against us with malicious words. And not content with that, he himself does not receive the brethren, and forbids those who wish to, putting them out of the church. Beloved, do not imitate what is evil, but what is good. He who does good is of God, but he who does evil has not seen God.* ~3 John 9-11

One Sunday morning after a great worship service, a woman and her husband approached me. The woman had been crying and was obviously angry, confused and upset. I had them follow me into my office so we could talk privately. They informed me that a woman in the church had been sending letters to people in the church. In these letters, she gave prophetic words from God. When they received and read one of these

SPIRIT WORLD

letters, they were greatly offended by rude and harsh words. The couple then asked me if I knew this was going on? I had no idea that someone had taken it upon herself to be a self-appointed prophet to the sheep I had been entrusted with. I asked to read the letter and was amazed at how rude it was. It was not the place of that woman to correct anyone else's faults. I assured the couple I would speak to this self-appointed prophetess.

I then found the matronly old woman who had been writing letters to parishioners. She informed me that this was her ministry and she called it like she saw it. I explained to her that prophecy in the New Testament is to be judged (see 1 Corinthians 14:29). I then asked her who is it that judges her prophecies? I told her that I needed her to let me read her prophetic letters before she sent them to members of the church. Her response kind of shocked me. Her face became red and she explained to me in no uncertain terms that she would not submit her letters or ministry to anyone. She told me that she was called by God alone and if her ministry was not received here at this church, she was taking it to another church. WOW!

I found out a couple of weeks later that she was attending another local church. The pastor assured me that she was in loving hands. Her new pastor insinuated that they were much more loving then me and were better equipped to nurture her. After all, she was such a sweet matronly ol' lady. Six months later, her pastor called me and was frustrated with her because she was writing scolding, prophetic letters to congregants. As much as I wanted to gloat about being right about this prophetess, I didn't. This was bad fruit that was being produced by this self-appointed judge. She was causing all kinds of problems and hurt feelings. Her rebellious nature demonstrated that she was not to be received as someone qualified to give prophetic words.

Desire to Prophesy

In the words of the Apostle John, *"Beloved, do not imitate what is evil, but what is good. He who does good is of God, but he who does evil has not seen God." (3 John 1:11). By their fruit you shall know them (Matthew 7:16).*

Remember the three tests of prophets and prophecies:

1. **Forthtelling:** Do they speak according to the Word of God?
2. **Foretelling:** Do they prophesy accurately?
3. **Fruit:** What is produced? What is the character of the prophet?

THE TRUE PROPHETIC IS BENEFICIAL

Now Judas and Silas, themselves being prophets also, exhorted and strengthened the brethren with many words.   ~Acts 15:32

Here we see that the true prophetic ministry exhorts and strengthens. Words prophesied from the heart of God will set people free. Darkness will turn to light and hopeless despondency will vanish with faith filled words of life. Out of our bellies should flow rivers of life. If our motives remain pure, not tainted with hidden agendas or self-exaltation, we will be a vessel of honor. God will speak through us to strengthen the brethren.

Folks often hear prophetic words from me, as their Pastor, but when a prophetic word comes from someone in the congregation it confirms that God is among us. This is similar in effect to great testimonies. When someone in the pews has a testimony to share, it shows that God is at work in everyone's life, not just the pastor's life.

I can't tell you how many times a prophetic word has come forth that confirmed the sermon for that service. Having no idea what I am going to teach and preach about, a prophet will exhort the church during the worship service, on the same theme. The Holy Spirit is confirming the word that is about to be preached. People will come up to me after the service and tell me how much the prophetic word and the sermon spoke to them. It wasn't just the sermon that comforted them, it was also the prophetic word.

> *Do not quench the Spirit. Do not despise prophecies. Test all things; hold fast what is good.* ~1 Thessalonians 5:19-21

> *Therefore, brethren, desire earnestly to prophesy, and do not forbid to speak with tongues. Let all things be done decently and in order.* ~1 Corinthians 14:39-40

PROPHETIC ETIQUETTE

> *Obey those who rule over you, and be submissive, for they watch out for your souls, as those who must give account. Let them do so with joy and not with grief, for that would be unprofitable for you.* ~Hebrews 13:17

If you are a prophetic person and desire to be used in your gifting, this section will help you. If you are a pastor and would like to nurture the prophetic gifts in your church, but are not sure how to manage them, then this section is for you as well.

When I speak of "prophetic etiquette," I'm speaking about being polite. I am also talking about the ground rules of your particular church. One size does not always fit all. There will be different rules for a big church as opposed to a smaller one. There will be different rules for a revival meeting as opposed to a regular Sunday morning worship service. There is one overriding rule of thumb that never changes, "Obey those who rule over you, and be submissive." The Pastor, or person in charge of the service, is the person who will give account to God. They are the gate keepers. They decide what the rules of the house are; what is allowed, and when. Since "they" (usually the pastor) are the ones who must someday stand before almighty God and explain their actions and give account for the state of the flock, it stands to reason that they are the ultimate authority in the service.

I once asked this question to some unruly folks in a church I pastored: "If the Holy Spirit is leading you to say or do something in the service and the Pastor says no, who do you obey?" Good question… "If God is telling the pastor one thing and you something else, who do you follow?" The answer is "THE PASTOR!" He/she's the one who has to give account to God, therefore he/she deserves the right to say yay, or nay. They are the gate keepers of what is allowed in the service. If they are wrong, God will deal with them, but someone has to be in charge; it's not a free-for-all.

I was hosting a conference at my church and the worship was over-the-top. I happened to be playing drums for that particular service and sometimes the worship leader cut the musicians loose and they flowed prophetically, spontaneously making up music as they played. I went to the low toms and was pounding out something that sounded very majestic and even warlike. When we were done, we sensed that God wanted to say something that tied into the prophetic worship we had just experienced. My wife Nicole, who was the worship leader for that meeting, asked a man that we knew sitting in the front row if he had anything from the Lord. The man strongly suggested that we should all start doing a Jericho march around the church.

Nicole looked to me for the final decision and I said "no." The reaction was weird. You could hear these whispering, shocked sighs sounding off throughout the small auditorium. When I sensed the hyper-sensitivity of the prophetic crowd, who were amazed that I would cut off the Holy Spirit, I realized that I should give a brief explanation. I explained that God is about to give us our marching order, and that that order was coming from our guest speaker, not through a prophetic act. That explanation seemed to suffice because the "how dare I" attitude evaporated and we went on to receive a great message from our guest speaker. The main thing that God wanted us to receive at that meeting was great preaching; THAT was the prophetic word for the hour. The man who suggested the Jericho march was hearing something that was right on, it was just the application that needed tweaking. If we had done the Jericho march around the sanctuary, it would have derailed what God was doing. The prophetic should never be allowed to highjack the service. The application of what God is saying and doing is the responsibility of the pastor, or whoever is in charge of the service.

There was another time our church hosted a series of revival meetings and other church pastors and members attended. During a lull in the worship a young woman asked to give a prophetic word. I knew her and she was a precious saint, so I agreed. Her word was very encouraging and very anointed, spot on. The problem was, she then took over the worship service and began leading us in song. She had a great voice and was a worship leader at the church she attended. The reason this was a problem was that she didn't ask permission for the song, and ended up highjacking the service. Use proper prophetic etiquette by always looking to the person in charge and asking permission. Chances are they will say yes, but if they say "no" don't be offended.

So, here's the rule: Submit to the person in charge of the service. Let the pastor give the application, or explanation of the prophetic word. Never take over the service by leading the folks in some action unless you have permission. Don't start preaching, don't lead us in song, and don't have an altar call, unless you get the go ahead from the leadership.

This can be difficult for prophetic people; they can be, by nature, a little rogue and eccentric. Keeping prophetic people moving in the same direction as the rest of the church can be a bit like herding cats.

> *Obey those who rule over you, and be submissive, for they watch out for your souls, as those who must give account.* ***Let them do so with joy and not with grief, for that would be unprofitable for you.***   ~Hebrews 13:17

Always double guessing the leadership and challenging them is unprofitable for you. Pray for your pastors, let them know that you love and support them. Give them grace. They do miss it from time to time, just like you. We are all growing up in the things of the Spirit together.

Here are my Prophetic Etiquette rules in the church I pastor:

1. Only members of our church can give a prophetic word. They can't be rogue people. They must be submitted to the local church and be in agreement with the basic doctrines and vision of the church. The exception is visiting spiritual leadership (i.e. missionaries, pastors and spiritually mature friends).

2. You must come up to the front of the church and wait to be acknowledged by the person in charge of the service. When giving your prophetic word, you must use the microphone designated for that purpose; we call it the prophecy microphone. This will allow everyone to hear the word given and ensure a proper flow of the service.

People feel safe with some pastoral guidelines. The only people who don't like it are the wolves; those who just want to flaunt themselves as super spiritual but don't have the best interest of the church in mind. As the shepherd of the sheep, you must answer to the Great Shepherd. Lovingly take charge. Nurture the prophetic in a safe environment.

SPIRIT WORLD

If correction must take place, try to do it privately first. If someone is openly rebellious, an open rebuke may be necessary that others may learn. Did I say that pastoring the prophetic is **a labor** of love? But it's worth it to receive amazing encouragement from the Lord.

> *Pursue love, and desire spiritual gifts, but especially that you may prophesy.* ~1 Corinthians 14:1

Chapter 12

SPIRITUAL ATMOSPHERES

Now thanks be to God who always leads us in triumph in Christ, and through us diffuses the fragrance of His knowledge in every place.   *~2 Corinthians 2:14*

THE FRAGRANCE OF HEAVEN

We are called to bring the fragrant atmosphere of heaven to this earth. We are containers of the Kingdom of God. Wherever we go, we create a spiritual atmosphere. The atmosphere of the Kingdom of God is righteousness, peace and joy in the Holy Spirit (see Romans 14:17). God's presence emanates life and healing. God's hope and faith replace despondency and fear. We are catalysts that change the spiritual atmosphere around us. We are NOT called to be **thermometers** that reflect the world's temperature. We ARE called to be **thermostats**, transforming the environment around us. The presence of demonic, spiritual darkness is vanquished when we walk into a room. We should never allow the presence of evil to overwhelm us, we should

SPIRIT WORLD

overwhelm it. This is why we need to be full of the Holy Spirit. When we are recharged, refreshed and ablaze with the Spirit of God, the power of God that transforms lives is manifest through us.

> *And do not be drunk with wine, in which is dissipation; but **be filled with the Spirit**, speaking to one another in psalms and hymns and spiritual songs, singing and making melody in your heart to the Lord.*   ~Ephesians 5:18-19

The life-giving fragrance of heaven remains on you after you leave the presence of God. Fill up during your private Bible reading and devotional times. Fill up in church services and at Bible studies. Fill up at prayer meetings and worship services. We must be full of grace to give grace.

There have been times when I could literally smell the fragrance of God's presence during our prayer/altar ministry times. Why would we think that is so strange? The Bible talks about seeing and hearing in the spirit, why not being able to smell spiritual aromas?

- King David was told that when he heard the sound of marching in the tops of the mulberry trees, that that would be the precise moment to advance on an enemy army (see 2 Samuel 5:22-25).
- Elisha asked God to open the eyes of his servant to see the protection of the angel armies around them (see 2 Kings 6:16-17).
- Paul prayed for the spiritual eyes of the church to be opened and enlightened, and able to see and comprehend the riches of Christ in all spiritual wisdom (see Ephesians 1:15-19).

What does the fragrance of heaven smell like? To me, it smelled like Christmas. At least what I experienced during the Christmas season as a child. It's the smell of my mother baking cookies and spicy sweet delicacies for a Christmas feast. It's the warm feeling of safety, security and being loved. It's the smell of allspice, cinnamon, sugar, and spices I can't identify, but I would know it if I smelled it.

In the book of Exodus, the bible gives the ingredients for the holy anointing oil and the holy incense (see Exodus 30:22-36). The children of Israel were forbidden to copy these aromatic concoctions for private use. There are sweet spices in those recipes that are unfamiliar to most of us; frankincense, stacte, onycha, and galbanum. I am told that these spices will disinfect the air when burned as incense. All airborne pathogens are eliminated. Not only is there a wonderful fragrance, but there is a cleansing of the atmosphere. This is what happens when we defuse the fragrance of the knowledge of God. The atmosphere around us is transformed and cleansed.

There was a time when a woman came to the altar and started to manifest a demonic oppression. How did I know she was manifesting a demonic force? When she started to contort her body in unnatural ways and hiss like a snake I got a clue. I'm not always the sharpest knife in the drawer, but my lightning fast brain figured that this was not the flesh, or God; this was devilish. She had been frequenting a native American sweat house and became demonized. As we were getting her set free, and the demonic stronghold began to loosen its grip on her, a sulfuric, rotten egg odor was emitted. This was the smell of death and the fragrance of Hell. There is a fragrance of life and one of death. You and I are to bring the atmosphere and aroma of heaven to every place we go.

> *For we are to God the fragrance of Christ among those who are being saved and among those who are perishing. To the one we are the aroma of death leading to death, and to the other the aroma of life leading to life. And who is sufficient for these things?* ~2 Corinthians 2:15-16

A PROPHETIC GOD ZONE

Then Saul sent messengers to take David. And when they saw the group of prophets prophesying, and Samuel standing as leader over them, the Spirit of God came upon the messengers of Saul, and they also prophesied. And when Saul was told, he sent other messengers, and they prophesied likewise. Then Saul sent messengers again the third time, and they prophesied also. ~1 Samuel 19:20-21

Samuel and his group of prophets were in a prophetic God zone. They were engulfed in the presence of God and caught up in the spirit of prophecy. Whenever someone came into close enough proximity to this God zone, they too were swept into prophetic bliss. Three times Saul sent messengers to arrest David, and three times they started prophesying right with Samuel and the group of prophets. Finally, King Saul himself went to arrest David and was also overwhelmed by this God zone. Saul began to prophesy and became lost in the spiritual atmosphere that was created.

I have been in meetings where a God zone was created. In some meetings, the spirit of prophecy would come down so powerfully that in that atmosphere anyone could prophesy. Folks that never had a prophetic revelation before were caught up in the God Zone and got very clear visions. There were times I could not get to my prepared sermon because God was speaking so profoundly through prophetic utterances. The Bible speaks of many kinds of prophetic utterances that can occur in a service. If there is proper oversight, things can transpire in a decent, orderly fashion. Samuel stood as leader over them. There must be mature, spiritual leadership conducting these meetings, steering things in an orderly fashion.

> *How is it then, brethren? Whenever you come together, each of you has a **psalm**, has a **teaching**, has a **tongue**, has a **revelation**, has an **interpretation**. Let all things be done for edification. If anyone speaks in a tongue, let there be two or at the most three, each in turn, and let one interpret. But if there is no interpreter, let him keep silent in church, and let him speak to himself and to God. **Let two or three prophets speak**, and let the others judge. But if anything is revealed to another who sits by, let the first keep silent. For you can all prophesy one by one, that all may learn and all may be encouraged. And the spirits of the prophets are subject to the prophets. For God is not the author of confusion but of peace, as in all the churches of the saints.* ~1 Corinthians 14:26-33

In the above verses, I emphasized several different kinds of prophetic expressions that can happen in a believer's meeting:

1. A psalm – A spontaneous prophetic song. A prophecy in song form; *"...be filled with the Spirit, speaking to one another in psalms and hymns and spiritual songs, singing and making melody in your heart to the Lord." (Ephesians 5:18b-19)*

2. A teaching – An on the spot, mini teaching that gives the "now" word from God. Someone will have one or two scripture verses to share with some insight.

3. A tongue with interpretation

4. A revelation – A divine insight, or vision; *"I will come to visions and revelations of the Lord." (2 Corinthians 12:1b)*

5. An interpretation – An interpretation of a tongue, or a sign, vision, or current event.

6. A prophecy – *"But he who prophesies speaks edification and exhortation and comfort to men." (1 Corinthians 14:3)*

Here I have given six different forms of prophetic expression that can happen in a believer's meeting. When a prophetic God zone drops, everyone is caught up in the experience.

I had a prejudice against these types of meetings where worship and the prophetic dominated. I heard a sermon called "The Primacy of the Pulpit." Even the name of the teaching sounds like religious bondage. I'm sure the guy who preached the message was sincere; he just didn't have a complete picture. The message was about how the preaching of the word should get priority over everything else in the service. He went so far as to say that if there is no sermon, the service is out of order. This made sense to me until I went to one particular all-night prayer meeting.

At this all-night prayer meeting, great worship, prophetic expressions and spontaneous prayers were the game plan. There wasn't a scheduled speaker per se, different leaders took turns leading the group in prayer. There were folks sharing visions and prophetic words all night. Early in the morning, I heard the Lord speak to my spirit in that familiar, still, small voice. "Did anyone have an organized sermon this entire night?" The obvious answer was "no." Then the question came to my spirit, "Did you receive revelation from my Word?" I received enough revelation to put together ten sermons. Even with the main focus of the meeting being prayer, the Word of God was always front and center. Every prophecy had the Word in it. Every vision was brought back to the Bible. Every prayer contained the Word of God. Just because a service doesn't have a structured sermon in it doesn't mean the Word of God is not a priority.

Please don't misunderstand me; the normal service should contain an organized message from a man or woman of God. I am just saying we should be open to the direction of the Holy Spirit. If a prophetic God zone opens up in your church meeting, go for it. The spiritual atmosphere of the kingdom of heaven is diverse. When God moves, move with Him.

A HEALING ATMOSPHERE

Now it happened on a certain day, as He was teaching, that there were Pharisees and teachers of the law sitting by, who had come out of every town of Galilee, Judea, and Jerusalem. ***And the power of the Lord was present to heal them.***
~Luke 5:17

We know theologically that God is omnipresent, or universally present, but there is a difference between the omnipresence of God and the manifest presence of God. At that particular meeting where Jesus was preaching, there was a powerful healing presence. There can be such a powerful healing atmosphere that healing virtue flows easily.

There are healing evangelists that carry with them a gift of faith, and gifts of healings. They bring with them an atmosphere of miraculous healing. Jesus carried this healing atmosphere with Him.

How God anointed Jesus of Nazareth with the Holy Spirit and with power, who went about doing good and ***healing all*** *who were oppressed by the devil, for God was with Him.*
~Acts 10:38

And Jesus went about all Galilee, teaching in their synagogues, preaching the gospel of the kingdom, and ***healing all*** *kinds of sickness and all kinds of disease among the people.*
~Matthew 4:23

Then Jesus went about all the cities and villages, teaching in their synagogues, preaching the gospel of the kingdom, and ***healing every sickness and every disease among the people****.*
~Matthew 9:35

Think about how awesome it would be to have a powerful healing presence fall in your Sunday morning church service where everyone is

SPIRIT WORLD

healed. Where every sickness, and every disease and infirmity afflicting God's people are vanquished. We always pray the prayer of faith at our altar ministry times and see some folks recover, but when a healing anointing drops, everyone gets healed; even those who do not come forward for prayer. Imagine worshiping in church, and as your hands are lifting in praise, pain leaves your body and you can literally feel the healing virtue flow into your body. This has happened and will happen more and more.

According to the Bible, WE have something to do with creating a powerful, transforming, spiritual atmosphere. I hate to be Delbert Downer, but we can also create a negative atmosphere where the Spirit of God is limited.

> *Now He could do no mighty work there, except that He laid His hands on a few sick people and healed them. And He marveled because of their unbelief. Then He went about the villages in a circuit, teaching.*
> *~Mark 6:5-6*

When we see a few sick folks healed, and a few people come up front to receive Jesus, we call it revival; Jesus called it an atmosphere of unbelief. We settle for under-whelming results when we should be expecting big things from a big God. What attitudes create a positive atmosphere?

1. **Be honoring:** Honor the leadership, honor one another. God can't move in an atmosphere where people are disrespectful to leadership and each other. Honor the Lord by giving Him respect and generous financial gifts. Honor God by coming to church ready to give the sacrifice of praise. Your hunger and expectant attitude pull virtue from heaven. Honor your parents in the Lord and honor your elders.

*Honor all people. Love the brotherhood. Fear God. Honor
the king.*   *~1 Peter 2:17*

*"Honor your father and mother," which is the first
commandment with promise: "that it may be well with you
and you may live long on the earth."*   *~Ephesians 6:2-3*

*You shall rise before the gray headed and honor the
presence of an old man, and fear your God: I am the LORD.*
                                                    ~Leviticus 19:32

*And we urge you, brethren, to recognize those who labor
among you, and are over you in the Lord and admonish you,
and to esteem them very highly in love for their work's sake.
Be at peace among yourselves.*   *~1 Thessalonians 5:12-13*

*Honor the LORD with your possessions,
And with the first fruits of all your increase;
So your barns will be filled with plenty,
And your vats will overflow with new wine.*
                                                    ~Proverbs 3:9-10

2. **Be loving:** We choose to love. We choose to be at peace with others. People that are always bickering, fighting and hostile are forfeiting the healing presence of God. Put down your pride. You don't always have to be right, or to have your own way. Forgive and let God deal with contrary people. For some folks, instead of a river of life flowing out of them it's a river of strife. I think it's their spiritual gift from hell. There is a reason the New Testament reminds us to love one another so many times, it's because we struggle.

*A new commandment I give to you, that you love one
another; as I have loved you, that you also love one*

another. By this all will know that you are My disciples, if you have love for one another."   *~John 13:34-35*

Let love be without hypocrisy. Abhor what is evil. Cling to what is good. Be kindly affectionate to one another with brotherly love, in honor giving preference to one another.
    ~Romans 12:9-10

With all lowliness and gentleness, with longsuffering, bearing with one another in love, endeavoring to keep the unity of the Spirit in the bond of peace.   *~Ephesians 4:2-3*

And above all things have fervent love for one another, for "love will cover a multitude of sins." Be hospitable to one another without grumbling.   *~1 Peter 4:8-9*

3. **Be expecting:** Come to every meeting expecting to hear and receive from God. Hungry people pull the loving hand of God down into the meeting. Apathetic, cynical people quench the Spirit. Instead of finding fault, look for God. Look for the blessing. Enough said. The woman with the flow of blood came expecting to be healed; she pressed in and received.

And suddenly, a woman who had a flow of blood for twelve years came from behind and touched the hem of His garment. For she said to herself, "If only I may touch His garment, I shall be made well." But Jesus turned around, and when He saw her He said, "Be of good cheer, daughter; your faith has made you well." And the woman was made well from that hour.   *~Matthew 9:20-22*

PRAYER CHANGES EVERYTHING

Confess your trespasses to one another, and pray for one another, that you may be healed. The effective, fervent prayer

Spiritual Atmospheres

> *of a righteous man avails much. Elijah was a man with a nature like ours, and he prayed earnestly that it would not rain; and it did not rain on the land for three years and six months. And he prayed again, and the heaven gave rain, and the earth produced its fruit.* ~James 5:16-18

Elijah was the supreme prayer warrior. Next to our Lord Jesus, Elijah was the Segundo of changing spiritual atmospheres through the power of prayer. He was just a man like you and me with flesh and blood, and yet he prayed that it would not rain for three-and-a-half years and it did not. Then he held a prayer competition on Mount Carmel where God answered by fire. There was no second and third place in this prayer competition, the prayer losers were to be killed and their god's abandoned (see 1 Kings 17-18).

Elijah changed the spiritual atmosphere of an entire nation through prayer and bravado. This should be a great encouragement to those of us who feel like lone voices of intercession in the night seasons. Elijah didn't have an intercessory team. He hadn't raised up a small army of prayer warriors that could grapple with the powers of darkness and turn back the enemy at the gate. He was alone. James holds up the prophet Elijah as an example that we should never be discouraged. If Elijah could change things through prayer, then so can we who are New Testament believers filled with the Holy Spirit. Read how James 5:16b speaks of prayer in the Amplified version of the Bible:

> *The earnest (heartfelt, continued) prayer of a righteous man makes tremendous power available [dynamic in its working].*
> ~James 5:16b AMP

In the above verse we find the elements of powerful, world-changing prayer: Earnestness, fervency, perseverance and righteousness. This will make tremendous power available, dynamic in its working.

- **"The earnest, heartfelt, continued prayer…"** This expresses a sincere, impassioned prayer. An enduring, persevering and tenacious prayer. *"I waited patiently for the LORD; and He inclined to me, and heard my cry." (Psalm 40:1).* When I think of tenacity and perseverance, I think of one of King David's mighty men, Eleazar (see 2 Samuel 23:9-10). The Philistines gathered in a field of lentils for battle and the men of Israel retreated. But not Eleazar, he stationed himself in the field and defeated, singlehandedly, a unit of the Philistine army. When the battle was over, and Eleazar had been victorious, they could not pry the sword from his hand. He was so frozen to the fight from all that hacking, thrusting, parrying and slashing, that his hand was locked to his weapon. That is tenacity. The Word of God is called the "sword of the spirit" (see Hebrews 4:12, Ephesians 6:17). We should be praying the Word of God with perseverance; slashing and stabbing in the spiritual realm, driving back the demonic hordes, until we are merged with our weapon.

- "The fervent prayer of a **righteous man** makes tremendous power available…" – We must make sure we are living right and our conscience is clear. *"If I regard iniquity in my heart, the Lord will not hear." (Psalm 66:18)* (see also Isaiah 59:1-2, 1 John 3:21-22). If your heart condemns you, ask forgiveness and keep short accounts with the Lord, and then put on the righteousness of Christ. You and I cannot approach the throne of grace based on our own righteousness, we have been made the righteousness of God in Christ! (see 2 Corinthians 5:21). Knowing that we are righteous in Christ is not an excuse to live sloppy; it is a never-ending source of confidence in receiving answers to your prayers.

- Also, a righteous man will always ask according to the Word of God. If you go to a taco stand, you can't ask for polish sausage and sauerkraut, you can only ask for what's on the menu. You can only pray according to the revealed will and character of God. This stands to reason that the more you know God and His Word, the more powerful your prayers will be. A righteous man will ask for righteous things.

- If these elements exist: earnestness, fervency, perseverance and righteousness, we can have confidence that God hears our prayers.

Beloved, if our heart does not condemn us, we have confidence toward God. And whatever we ask we receive from Him, because we keep His commandments and do those things that are pleasing in His sight.
~1 John 3:21-23

Not all of us are on that level where we are transforming the spiritual atmospheres of entire nations by the forcefulness of our prayers. But what about transforming the atmosphere of your work, home, church and school? What about influencing your community, county and state? I believe you and I are more powerful and influential than we know.

I was on staff as a Youth Pastor and our church called a special prayer meeting. Our church needed a spiritual breakthrough; we needed to be more "on fire." We had slumped into a dry and apathetic place. (At least we recognized our need, some churches keep hobbling on in that dry state until they blindly stumble over a cliff into oblivion.) At least 25 people arrived to press in for a measure of revival. The lights in the sanctuary were turned down low and the dirge music was pensive. At first, I thought we were at a funeral service rather than at a prayer meeting for fervent revival. Maybe we should just lay the church to rest in a shallow grave and all move on with our lives?

SPIRIT WORLD

The music eventually kicked up a bit and eventually became almost warlike. I was in front of everyone, facing the cross on the podium, when God's still small voice spoke to me. "Will you dance for me?" I immediately began testing the spirits to see if this was God. Why would God ask me to dance for Him? I'm not a dancer. I would look like a complete idiot and make a fool of myself if I started dancing at this dead prayer meeting. It might be easier to dance at a big hipster worship service where all the young people up front are jumping up and down, but not here. The Lord heard the conflict going on in my heart and repeated the question, "Would you dance for ME?" The emphasis was a little more on the "ME" this time. It was kind of like God was asking if I loved Him enough to make a fool of myself. Well, I decided I did love God enough to dance for him so I started dancing.

As I stepped out in faith and started dancing, the Spirit of God came over me and I began doing a warlike, native American dance. It was very fervent. It was like I was interceding through the dance. I must have jumped, bounced and gyrated like that for five to ten minutes until I was very sweaty and out of breath. Then the Spirit of God spoke to me and told me to turn around and look. As I began to turn around, I expected everyone to be staring at the Youth Pastor who was having a nervous breakdown in living color right in front of them. Instead, everyone was leaping and dancing. It was wild pandemonium. Everyone was caught up in the fervor of the Spirit. The heavens were open and vitality was once again being poured out onto our church.

Afterwards, folks were asking me how I could dance like that? It was awesome! There was such a glory coming off of me as I made war with the dance. To this day I have not danced like that again.

God wants to use you to transform spiritual atmospheres from a smothering death to living vitality, from confusion to clarity, from despondency to joy, from darkness and oppression, to light and freedom. Let me close this chapter with just a few of my favorite Bible verses that promise answers to prayer. Prayer changes everything.

> I sought the LORD, and He heard me,
> And delivered me from all my fears.
> They looked to Him and were radiant,
> And their faces were not ashamed.
> This poor man cried out, and the LORD heard him,
> And saved him out of all his troubles.
> The angel of the LORD encamps all around those who fear
> Him, And delivers them. ~Psalm 34:4-7

> Most assuredly, I say to you, he who believes in Me, the works that I do he will do also; and greater works than these he will do, because I go to My Father. And whatever you ask in My name, that I will do, that the Father may be glorified in the Son. If you ask anything in My name, I will do it.
> ~John 14:12-14

> Be anxious for nothing, but in everything by prayer and supplication, with thanksgiving, let your requests be made known to God; and the peace of God, which surpasses all understanding, will guard your hearts and minds through Christ Jesus. ~Philippians 4:6-7

> Now this is the confidence that we have in Him, that if we ask anything according to His will, He hears us. And if we know that He hears us, whatever we ask, we know that we have the petitions that we have asked of Him. ~1 John 5:14-15

The Bible teaches that we are in an epic, cosmic conflict; grappling with evil spiritual beings for dominance in the earthly and heavenly realms.

Chapter 13

SPIRITUAL WARFARE

Finally, my brethren, be strong in the Lord and in the power of His might. Put on the whole armor of God, that you may be able to stand against the wiles of the devil. For we do not wrestle against flesh and blood, but against principalities, against powers, against the rulers of the darkness of this age, against spiritual hosts of wickedness in the heavenly places.
~Ephesians 6:10-12

What do you think of when you hear the term "spiritual warfare?" The first thing that would come to my mind is angel armies preparing for war. A desolate landscape with a gunmetal grey sky backdrop. Two ferocious battle fronts facing each other with a craggy ground in between. The angels of darkness on one side, led by their general Lucifer, also known as the prince of darkness. The angels of light on the other side, led by the Archangel Michael. As the battle lines collide, there is the sickening sound of impact as metal shields, helmets, and swords mash. The concussive impact of supernatural armies colliding causes shock waves through the heavens and earth. Okay, I may be over dramatic, but there truly IS a spiritual, intergalactic war in progress. What part do we mere humans have to play in this clash of immortal titans?

The Bible teaches that we are in an epic, cosmic conflict; grappling with evil spiritual beings for dominance in the earthly and heavenly realms. Pretending that malevolent, demonic hordes don't exist and that everything is just hunky-dory is pure deception and ignorance to what the Bible teaches. This spiritual war is fought on three fronts: (1) The world system (anti-Christ culture), (2) the flesh (evil desires within), (3) and on a spiritual level with the Devil (Satan, Lucifer, the prince of the power of the air) and his fallen angels (demons). The keys to winning on all three battle fronts are the same: **obedience, truth, knowing your authority, and fighting from a position of victory**. These four areas are the strategic high ground in spiritual warfare. Unless you have good footing and a strong foundation from which to fight, the spiritual weapons of our warfare are useless. By spiritual weapons, I'm referring to things like: the name of Jesus, the word of your testimony, the blood of Jesus, praying in the Spirit, and so forth. For example, if I am not living under God's authority, or knowing my authority as a believer, invoking the mighty name of Jesus to tell a spirit of fear to go will not work.

I find it interesting that the above verse (Ephesians 6:10-12) uses the term "wrestle" when describing the intimate hand-to-hand combat of spiritual warfare. In most American High Schools, we use Freestyle, or Folk style wrestling. The Greco-Roman style that Paul was familiar with was much more violent then what we have today. When pinning your opponent to the ground is the goal, most contests are NOT quick wins. You must wear down your opponent; it becomes a battle of attrition and endurance. So it is with spiritual warfare; you must be tenacious, unyielding, relentless and totally reliant on the strength of the Lord.

Spiritual Warfare

Most battles are not quick, easy wins. You may have to take the high ground many times before you hold it and advance to new territory.

For a righteous man may fall seven times and rise again, but the wicked shall fall by calamity. ~Proverbs 24:16

You may be in a battle right now and have experienced some setbacks. Don't quit! Don't settle for anything less than total victory. You may have stumbled again and again, but don't give up! You are better today than you were yesterday. Though you fall seven times, rise up again. By being tenacious you will ultimately have the victory dance. Stand your ground. Don't be pushed around. Push back.

In the screen movie, "The Untouchables," the FBI is at war with the Chicago gangsters circa 1920's, namely Al Capone. A tough, seasoned Irish cop by the name of Jim Malone, played by Sean Connery, gives some advice to the young Eliot Ness. "You wanna get Capone? Here's how you get him. He pulls a knife, you pull a gun. He sends one of yours to the hospital, you send one of his to the morgue! That's the Chicago way." In spiritual warfare you have to keep coming back harder until you wear your opponent down and pin him to the ground. You CAN win if you never give up.

And the God of peace will crush Satan under your feet shortly. The grace of our Lord Jesus Christ be with you. Amen.
~Romans 16:20

But thanks be to God, who gives us the victory through our Lord Jesus Christ. Therefore, my beloved brethren, be steadfast, immovable, always abounding in the work of the Lord, knowing that your labor is not in vain in the Lord.
~1 Corinthians 15:57-58

> *Watch, stand fast in the faith, be brave, be strong.*
> ~*1 Corinthians 16:13*

OBEDIENCE IS THE KEY TO VICTORY

> *Therefore submit to God. Resist the devil and he will flee from you.*
> ~*James 4:7*

Notice that submission to God is the first step toward resisting the devil. Demons will not obey you if you are NOT under God's authority. **You must be under authority to have authority.** God's spiritual authority is delegated to those who are obedient. If you are not submitted to God you have no kingdom authority. We could talk of all the assorted weapons of spiritual warfare: the blood of the Lamb, the word of your testimony, the name of Jesus, praying in the Spirit, declaring the word of God, and so forth; but all these amazing things are useless to you if you are in rebellion.

When you are racing over the speed limit and you hear sirens and see flashing lights coming from the police car in your rear-view mirror, you are compelled to pull your automobile over to the side of the road. Why do you have to obey that officer? Because he represents a higher authority than himself. Backing him up is a whole army of blue Smurfs, and they all have guns. The police officer has authority because he is acting under authority. His job is to uphold the law; to serve and protect the community from anarchy. When he is acting in an official capacity, the powers of the government back him up. If some yahoo tried to pull you over with his rusty pick-up truck and a yellow flashing light on top of his cab that he bought at Wal-Mart, you would laugh and keep going. This is the difference between you acting in your own authority or acting

Spiritual Warfare

under submission to the kingdom of God. When you are under the authority of the kingdom, all the powers of Heaven back you up.

The Bible says that rebellion is as the sin of witchcraft (see 1 Samuel 15:23). To be living in obstinate rebellion and presume to use the name of Jesus to take authority over the demonic is laughable. It's like a three-year-old toddler telling his parents to shut up and make him a sandwich. It's like the seven sons of Sceva who tried to use the name of Jesus to cast out a devil. Without knowing Jesus or being under His authority, the demon possessed man leaped on them and beat them until they were naked and bleeding (see Acts 19:14). You will stand no chance resisting the devil until you are submitted to God.

The first and best act of spiritual warfare is simply to OBEY GOD! Many spiritual attacks would cease as soon as you obey. Just to be clear, I am NOT saying that all bad things that happen to you are the result of you being in disobedience in some area of your life. You can be doing everything right and the devil will try to attack you. The devil is a bully who will go after the timid. He will push you around if he thinks he can get away with it. But there are many problems and trials that come upon us because of our rebellion. A brutally honest self-evaluation is always in order before we go to war. Don't go into battle unless you are under God's authority and clothed in the righteousness of Christ. The demonic will not recognize your authority, but they will submit to the authority of Christ operating through you. Acknowledge and confess your rebellion to the Lord.

> *If we confess our sins, He is faithful and just to forgive us our sins and to cleanse us from all unrighteousness. If we say that we have not sinned, we make Him a liar, and His word is not in us.* ~1 John 1:9-10

SPIRIT WORLD

> *He who covers his sins will not prosper, but whoever confesses and forsakes them will have mercy.* ~Proverbs 28:13

A minister friend of mine was planning an evangelistic trip to India. He was partnering with another minister, and they had raised enough money through conferences and meetings held across the country. My friend was very excited to go. Connections were established in India. Halls, churches and open-air fields were being arranged for the upcoming meetings. All the logistics and planning were underway.

A couple weeks before they were to fly out, it was revealed that my friend's partner in the endeavor was having an affair with his secretary. Immediately, my minister friend canceled everything. All the contacts in India were through this man having the adulterous affair. Everything came crashing down. My friend said to me, "India is a place of great oppression and spiritual warfare. There is no way I am going into that kind of intense warfare with someone who is in rebellion against God." He knew it would be a colossal failure without the blessing and anointing of God to break every yoke of demonic oppression.

> *If you are **willing and obedient**,*
> *You shall eat the good of the land;*
> *But if you refuse and rebel,*
> *You shall be devoured by the sword"*
> *For the mouth of the LORD has spoken.* ~Isaiah 1:19-20

As a young family sat down at the dinner table, their three-year-old toddler was set down into the high chair. As the Mom was bringing the food to the table, the toddler wiggled his way to a standing position in the high chair. The Dad did not have to be a prophet to foresee the immediate future; this kid could easily flip out of the chair and hurt himself badly, thus, ruining the dinner (I hate it when that happens). He commanded the child to "sit down!"

The child's response was, "NO!", to which the father quickly got up from his chair, marched over to the high chair, and forced the toddler down into a sitting position. The child began to cry loudly and said, "I'm standing on the inside!"

Outward conformity to God and His word is not enough. We cannot give God just mere lip service and inwardly be resentful of His restraints. *"The backslider in heart will be filled with his own ways, but a good man will be satisfied from above." (Proverbs 14:14)*. The heart that is meditating on rebellion will eventually act on those desires. If you are **willing and obedient,** you will eat the good of the land.

TRUTH IS A MIGHTY SPIRITUAL WEAPON

Then Jesus said to those Jews who believed Him, "If you abide in My word, you are My disciples indeed. And you shall know the truth, and the truth shall make you free." ~John 8:31-32

Truth... "What is truth?" This is what Pilate said to Christ (see John 18:38). He wasn't really asking, it was meant to be a rhetorical question. In Pilate's mind, there was no absolute truth, only the truth that every man lived by. Whatever got you through the day and helped you survive, that was truth to Pilate. Jesus told Pilate that He came to bear witness to the truth, and everyone who is of the truth hears Him (see John 18: 38). To the Christian, truth is absolute and eternal. It's not subject to social mores or the ever-shifting cultural values of a society. It's bigger than our biases, personal perspective, prejudices, warped values and altered view of reality. It goes far beyond our limited understanding. Pilate asked, "What is truth?" and he did not comprehend that the embodiment of truth was standing right in front of him. Jesus said, *"I am the way, the truth, and the life. No one comes to the Father except through me." (John 14:6)*.

SPIRIT WORLD

Jesus is the absolute truth at the exclusion of all others. Jesus, Buddha, and Mohammad cannot all be true. Two polar opposites cannot both be true. Jesus did not leave you with any options. If Jesus said that He is the truth, and the only way to God, then the case is closed. Jesus backed up His claim with credentials; He had over 300 prophecies written in a 1,500-year time span that predicted His existence as a human being. Prophecies that were literally fulfilled; about where He would be born, where He would live, how He would die, and that He would die for the sins of mankind. The odds of all those prophecies being fulfilled in one man are so astronomical that you are a fool not to consider it. His sinless life, the miracles he performed, and the greatest miracle of all: raising Himself from the dead. These credentials are not found in any of the other candidates. As a matter of fact, Christianity is the only religion that offers a relationship with the living God. All other religions offer a system of works that *might* bring some sort of salvation, but nothing is guaranteed because their god is a mystery and his will is a mystery. While promising freedom, or enlightenment, they put their adherents into more bondage.

I was taking guitar lessons from a Venezuelan master musician, and my daughter, who was about 12 at the time, was sitting with another young man her age. As they talked and waited for me to get done, the conversation progressed and my daughter asked him what church he went to? He said that he went to a church that believed in the unity of all religions and that there are many roads that lead to heaven. My daughter responded, "That doesn't make sense. There is only one road that goes to my house. I'm hungry. I want to get home and eat. I don't want to be wandering around looking for the right road." Ha-ha, I laughed under my breath. They didn't realize that I had one ear on their conversation and one ear on my guitar instructor. If you want to get to heaven, make sure you're on the right road; His name is Jesus. The right road map is the 66 books of the Holy Bible.

God's Word is compared to seed in the Bible (see Luke 8:11, 1 Peter 1:23). The truth of the Bible is so powerful that it will grow mightily and prevail over lies and deception. It will grow mightily and prevail over negative thinking and mental strongholds. It will even overpower poverty and sickness. Almost everything in life starts out in seed form. Every seed produces after its own kind. In the seed of an acorn is the DNA construct of an Oak tree. It doesn't become an oak tree overnight; it grows over time. The truth of God's Word is the seed that will not return void, or empty. It will grow mightily and bring freedom. The truth will set you free. The truth of the word of God is a spiritual thing, because it comes from a spiritual source, the Holy Spirit (see 2 Peter 1:20-21). Therefore, it is an indestructible seed. God's word will accomplish what He sends it forth to do.

> *So the word of the Lord grew mightily and prevailed.*
> *~Acts 19:20*

> *So shall My word be that goes forth from My mouth;*
> *It shall not return to Me void,*
> *But it shall accomplish what I please,*
> *And it shall prosper in the thing for which I sent it.*
> *~Isaiah 55:11*

The truth of God's word is a powerful spiritual force that will tear down strongholds of intricate deception. The truth of God's word is the sword of the Spirit, cutting away at the lies that bombard your mind. Lies destroy, but truth brings hope and life.

> *The weapons we fight with are not the weapons of the world. On the contrary, they have divine power to demolish strongholds. We demolish arguments and every pretension*

SPIRIT WORLD

that sets itself up against the knowledge of God, and we take captive every thought to make it obedient to Christ.
~2 Corinthians 10:4-5 NIV

One of my first jobs was washing dishes in a restaurant. Many times I was paired up with another teenager who carried a Gideon's New Testament with Psalms and Proverbs in his back pocket. I became his personal evangelistic project. *I believed a lie that it didn't matter how much you sinned as long as you asked for forgiveness. God understands that we are sinners, that's why Jesus died for us. All you have to do is believe in Jesus to be saved.* After bantering for a month, he finally cut to the chase. He was going to let me have it with some very inconvenient truths that would attack my compromised lifestyle.

First of all, he asked, "You say you believe; did you know that demons believe as well? The Bible says in James 2:19-20, *"You believe that there is one God. You do well. Even the demons believe — and tremble! But do you want to know, O foolish man, that faith without works is dead?"* The demons believe in God more than you, they have even seen God. Let me ask you this; are the demons going to heaven? After all, they do believe... NO, of course not. So, there are different levels of belief. You can believe that George Washington was our first president and that Jesus died on a cross for the sins of the world; this is a mental assent to historical facts, not saving faith. Peter and the disciples left ALL to follow Jesus. What have you given up? Jesus said in the Book of Revelation 'I know your works, that you are neither cold nor hot. I could wish you were cold or hot. So then, because you are lukewarm, and neither cold nor hot, I will vomit you out of My mouth' (see Revelation 3:15-16). If you are lukewarm, you are NOT going to heaven. Jesus said He would vomit you out of His mouth."

WOW! This was quite the little sermon. It hit home. I was totally located. Holy conviction set in and the indestructible seed of God's word was planted in my heart. Although outwardly I did not show it, inwardly I was shaken to the core. For five long years I was tormented with these verses. Every time I went to a drunken party, I would hear in my spirit a whisper of conviction, "You are lukewarm. You are lukewarm neither hot nor cold. You are living a lie, pretending to be a Christian and living a compromised lifestyle."

Finally, the seed of truth grew mightily and prevailed over my personal theology of compromise. At the age of 21, I couldn't take it anymore. I went down to the altar and committed my life to Christ; I became born again.

> *Then Jesus said to those Jews who believed Him, "If you abide in My word, you are My disciples indeed. And you shall know the truth, and the truth shall make you free."* ~John 8:31-32

Never underestimate the power of the truth of God's Word. You can deliver yourself just by continuing in the truth of God's word. The truth is greater that the facts of your circumstances. In the book of Numbers, chapter 13, twelve spies were sent into the land of Canaan to bring back a report of the land. Ten of the spies gave an "evil, or bad" report of the land (see Numbers 13:27-32). They told it like it was and declared a factual account of what they saw. The land did indeed flow with abundant provision but the cities were well fortified with high, impregnable walls, and there were giants in the land. From a factual standpoint it seemed impossible to conquer this land. Joshua and Caleb also spied the land with the other ten spies and their perception was different. They were looking through the eyes of faith. The truth of God's promises was greater than the facts of the circumstances. God said He would be with them and fight for them. Things that are impossible with man are possible WITH God. Whose report will you believe? We will believe the report of the Lord. We will let the Lord have the last Word, and that is what we will believe.

> *But Jesus looked at them and said, "With men it is impossible, but not with God; for with God all things are possible."*
> ~Mark 10:27

YOU HAVE AUTHORITY OVER THE DEMONIC

> *Behold, I give you the authority to trample on serpents and scorpions, and over all the power of the enemy, and nothing shall by any means hurt you.* ~Luke 10:19

When I was a youth pastor, I wanted to create a discipleship program that would be bad to the bone. I came up with this Idea of an Impossible Mission Force; the IMF, obviously taken from the Mission Impossible movies. A small group of eight students gathered in the classroom for the first lesson.

I explained that I wanted to create a group of devil stomping, tongue talking, Jesus freaks. "I'm going to be hard on you. Some of you won't make it. You will either quit, or get booted out. This will be Special Forces training for Christian leadership. After I give my expectations, any, or all of you, are welcome to back out today. I will love you just the same if you decide not to go through with this training. If you quit, you will always be accepted in the youth group but you will not be IMF."

I went on to tell them that we were starting out with a thirty-day ALL Media fast. No computers or internet except for homework. No television. No video games. No social media. Phones will only be permitted for communication and reading online books. I lost several students in the first couple weeks who couldn't keep the media fast.

At the beginning of every session I made them stand up and pray loudly in tongues until we felt a spiritual breakthrough. Usually we would pray for fifteen or twenty minutes. A great peace would settle over the group and some of them would prophesy for the first time. At the end of our prayer times some would weep uncontrollably as the Holy Spirit washed and delivered them from oppression. The love of God poured all over those kids. They had text book and Bible reading assignments as well.

I wanted them fearless in the face of demonic attack, so Luke 10:19 became our theme verse. Jesus has given us authority over serpents and scorpions; these are emblems of evil spirits. *"And nothing shall by any means harm you."* When you are under the protection of the blood of Jesus and acting in His authority, you are God's Impossible Mission Force. Jesus came to destroy the works of the devil, and we are training to carry out His work (see 1 John 3:8).

During one of our regular youth nights at the church, as I was preaching a young man in the front row started growling at me. I looked at another young man on my IMF team seated a couple seats over, and we both shrugged at each other. The question in my eyes was, "Did we just hear him growl?" I went on with my preaching and the kid growled at me again. A discernment buzzer started going off in my spirit and I knew I was dealing with a demonic manifestation. (I don't really hear a buzzer in my spirit; it's a figure of speech. LOL)

I bent over and looked at him directly in the eyes. The eyes are the window to the soul. A demon peered back at me and he saw that I was not intimidated or afraid. The young man possessed with the demon jumped up and ran for the door. I yelled out "IMF don't let him leave. GET HIM!" Three guys tackled him and chairs went everywhere. Pandemonium broke out as scared young people ran for the door to get away from a demon manifesting. This 110-pound kid with whistle stick arms was being held down by four guys and still he was lifting some off the ground.

As I walked up to the scene, the demon possessed boy calmed down a bit. We looked each other in the eyes and he began saying vile things to me and threatening to kill my family. He looked at one of the young men holding him down and told him that he was at the car accident several years ago that almost killed him. The demon inside the boy peered at the young man and said, "I was there at that accident and I was trying to kill you." It was impossible for that boy to know anything about that accident. The demon inside the boy knew things and knew how to psychologically intimidate. But we knew Luke 10:19, *"Behold, I give you the authority to trample on serpents and scorpions, and over all the power of the enemy, and nothing shall by any means hurt you."* **Nothing shall by any means hurt you!**

We knew our authority over devils. I did what Jesus did in the Bible and commanded the demon to not speak. I then commanded to speak to the boy and not to the demon. The boy then confessed that he had been dabbling in Satanism and I led him in a prayer of repentance. He then renewed his vow to serve Jesus and after that it was easy to command the demon to leave. That devil had no legal right to demonize that boy any longer.

The lesson here is to know who you are in Christ. You must be confident in your authority as a Christian. Christians put up with far too many shenanigans from demons. Use the name of Jesus; His name is the Christian's Power of Attorney. Tell demonic oppression to GO in the mighty name of Jesus. And when you've done all to stand, STAND longer! Some would say, "It can't be that easy." It is!

The power of the Kingdom of Heaven backs you up because you are under God's protection.

> *The name of the LORD is a strong tower; the righteous run to it and are safe.* ~Proverbs 18:10

> *Nor is there salvation in any other, for there is no other name under heaven given among men by which we must be saved.* ~Acts 4:12

> *Therefore God also has highly exalted Him and given Him the name which is above every name, that at the name of Jesus every knee should bow, of those in heaven, and of those on earth, and of those under the earth.* ~Philippians 2:9-10

FIGHTING FROM A POSITION OF VICTORY

> *Having disarmed principalities and powers, He made a public spectacle of them, triumphing over them in it.* ~Colossians 2:15

> *Inasmuch then as the children have partaken of flesh and blood, He Himself likewise shared in the same, that through death He might destroy him who had the power of death, that is, the devil, and release those who through fear of death were all their lifetime subject to bondage.* ~Hebrews 2:14-15

In 1991, the United States declared war against Iraq. The code name for the war was Operation Desert Storm. The brief war also earned the nickname "Video Game War" because it was the first war we could watch live on cable news. American General, Norman Schwarzkopf, became internationally famous for his brilliant strategy in leading the coalition forces to a quick victory. First, he bombed all communication centers so Iraq's central command couldn't communicate with its armies. Then he destroyed all the enemy air support to maintain air superiority. After destroying all bridges and ways for the enemy to re-supply, he cut them off and overran the nation. The whole operation began on January 17th, 1991, and lasted just five weeks. Even though the U.S. had won the war, we didn't push an unconditional surrender. The objective was to liberate the nation of Kuwait from Iraq occupation. Saddam Hussein and his corrupt regime were allowed to continue causing unrest in the Middle East. We never occupied the land we liberated.

In March of 2003, the U. S. invaded Iraq again in what was dubbed "Operation Iraqi Freedom." This invasion lasted from March 20th, to May 1st. Just five weeks and four days. This time we completely overthrew the existing government and occupied the country. The mission changed from invasion to occupation. This new mission was called "Operation Enduring Freedom." Although the initial victory and toppling of the government took a very short time, occupation and rebuilding has been costly. This is so much like the spiritual war we are in now. Jesus won the war. He triumphed over the wicked spiritual forces of this world. You and I are now the clean-up crew, ferreting out pockets of resistance. We are trying to maintain Kingdom rule over our lives and resisting attempts by the enemy to pull us back into darkness.

Jesus has already won the war! We fight from a position of victory!

The children of Israel were given title deed to the Promised Land. It was theirs by a covenant of Salt. God told them He would be with them and help them possess the land. Although the cities were walled and there were giants in the land, God fought for them. God caused walls to collapse with a shout. He caused great hail stones to fall on the enemy. Everywhere they turned, the enemy was routed. No man stood before Joshua all the days of his life. If they wanted territory, they simply had

Spiritual Warfare

to mobilize and go take it. The conquest of Canaan is a type of Jesus leading us into victory. If we follow Jesus, He will always lead us to victory.

> *But thanks be to God, who gives us the victory through our Lord Jesus Christ.* ~1 Corinthians 15:57

> *Now thanks be to God who always leads us in triumph in Christ, and through us diffuses the fragrance of His knowledge in every place.* ~2 Corinthians 2:14

Many times I have felt defeated, but there is a victory to achieve out of every situation. Somehow, Jesus can still get a victory. He **always** leads me to triumph. Nothing can work against me but only for me. He causes all thing to work together for my good (see Romans 8:28). I've seen the death of a loved one lead to hundreds hearing the Gospel. Setbacks have been turned into opportunities. Great tests have turned into amazing testimonies.

Another way that we fight from a position of victory is that we must stand in the righteousness of Christ. If you are always feeling condemned, you are not going to be confident in your spiritual authority. Condemnation and sin consciousness will destroy faith every time. You will always feel unworthy for God's blessings and victorious life. When you become a Christian, your life is hidden in Christ. The epistles of Paul constantly speak about what we are "in Christ."

> *For He made Him who knew no sin to be sin for us, that we might become the righteousness of God in Him.*
> ~2 Corinthians 5:21

We don't approach God in our own self-righteousness. We can never be good enough to have a friendship with God. That's why we need to be "in Christ." Some people behave better than others, but we all fall short.

SPIRIT WORLD

If a thousand people started to swim from Surfrider Beach in Malibu, California, and attempted to make it all the way to Hawaii, some would get further than others, but all would become shark bait. *"All have sinned and fall short of the glory of God" (Romans 3:23).* No one makes it on their own righteousness.

If you are feeling convicted about any sin, confess it and get right with God before you go to war. Don't give the devil any foothold to condemn you and challenge your authority. You must also be willing to turn from what you know is wrong with God's help.

> *If we confess our sins, He is faithful and just to forgive us our sins and to cleanse us from all unrighteousness. If we say that we have not sinned, we make Him a liar, and His word is not in us.* ~1 John 1:9-10

> *He who covers his sins will not prosper,*
> *But whoever confesses and forsakes them will have mercy.*
> ~Proverbs 28:13

Some preachers are always trying to make you feel unworthy and condemned. I call it sin consciousness preaching. In their zeal to make sure folks grasp their need for Christ, they never explain that when you are found in Christ you become righteous. You become clothed in Christ's righteousness. You now stand forgiven, washed, and cleansed. *What can wash my sins away? Nothing but the blood of Jesus.* This is the moral high ground you posses in Jesus. You are fighting from a position of victory, not condemnation. When you are in the midst of a spiritual battle and your mind is filled with thoughts of unworthiness, don't just sit there and take it. Quote 2 Corinthians 5:21 and then say, "I am the righteousness of God in Christ Jesus! Back off Mr. Devil!"

> *For if our heart condemns us, God is greater than our heart, and knows all things. Beloved, if our heart does not condemn*

us, we have confidence toward God. And whatever we ask we receive from Him, because we keep His commandments and do those things that are pleasing in His sight. ~1 John 3:19-22

STRENGTH FOR THE BATTLE

Listed below are some of my favorite Bible verses for supernatural strength. I never claim to be strong enough on my own to face life's challenges. Without faith and trust in God I would be easily broken. God wants to empower you with supernatural strength. Declare these verses when you are feeling overwhelmed. When you are weak, then you are strong, because you are wrapping yourself up in God's unlimited strength and power.

I have strength for all things in Christ Who empowers me [I am ready for anything and equal to anything through Him Who infuses inner strength into me; I am self-sufficient in Christ's sufficiency]. ~Philippians 4:13 AMP

*In the day when I cried out, you answered me,
And made me bold with strength in my soul.* ~Psalm 138:3

*The LORD is my light and my salvation; whom shall I fear?
The LORD is the strength of my life; of whom shall I be afraid?*
~Psalm 27:1

Have I not commanded you? Be strong and of good courage; do not be afraid, nor be dismayed, for the LORD your God is with you wherever you go. ~Joshua 1:9

*It is God who arms me with strength, and makes my way perfect.
He makes my feet like the feet of deer, and sets me on my high places.*

SPIRIT WORLD

He teaches my hands to make war, so that my arms can bend a bow of bronze.
~Psalm 18:32-34

He gives power to the weak, and to those who have no might He increases strength.
Even the youths shall faint and be weary, and the young men shall utterly fall, but those who wait on the LORD shall renew their strength; they shall mount up with wings like eagles, they shall run and not be weary, they shall walk and not faint.
~Isaiah 40:29-31

The spirit world is real, and we need the spiritual strength of the Lord to live the abundant life. My prayer is that this book has helped equip you to live victorious, discerning and aware. You are loved. You are valuable. Welcome to the war. Fight the good fight of faith. It's always a good fight when you can win, and you can win. Believe in the unseen for it is real.

Jesus said to him, "Thomas, because you have seen Me, you have believed. Blessed are those who have not seen and yet have believed."
~John 20:29

Radical Transformation

Therefore, if anyone is in Christ, he is a new creation; old things have passed away; behold, all things have become new.
~*2 Corinthians 5:17 NKJV*

Can a person change?

When I was 21 years old, I played drums for a bar band in Saginaw Michigan. One night after the gig, the drunken bash moved from the night club to a home. My friend dragged me out of the party because I was causing trouble and he was afraid that a couple guys would jump me and clean my clock (something I probably deserved). On the way home we missed a turn and our car smashed head on into the face of a ditch. I woke up in the hospital emergency room with a bruised face and my upper and lower jaws were broken in seven places. While recuperating at home with my jaws wired shut, I was contemplating what a loser I was and wondered; "If I had died in that wreck would I have gone to hell?" One day as I was thinking on heaven and hell and the existence of God, a knock came on the door; it was a friend that I hadn't seen in a year or so. He told me about how he had given his life

SPIRIT WORLD

to Christ and then invited me to go to church with him that night. God's timing was amazing. Here I was, in a low place and questioning everything about my life and God sends a witness.

At the service that night I made my way to the front of the church and committed my life to Christ. A fellow came over to me, put his hand on my back and prayed with me. He then spoke 2 Corinthians 5:17 to me, *"If anyone is in Christ, he is a new creation; old things have passed away; behold, all things have become new."* I can't explain to you how much hope that verse brought to me. My life would be changed now. I would have a new beginning and fresh start. God would help me change the direction of my life.

The transformation was so radical and severe that it put a fright into some of my friends and family. Some thought I was having an emotional breakdown (something that did happen when I was 17 just after my parents divorced). Some thought I had been deceived into joining a fanatical religious cult. My Dad even bought me a book on cults and told me to see if I was in there. Some of this was pretty humorous to me. I quit drinking alcohol, drugs and cigarettes cold turkey. My language had been so vile and filthy that I could not use one sentence without cussing. I had to retrain myself in speaking the English language. I would catch myself just before letting a revolting word slip out. My speech was strange, broken and stuttered for a while as I kept stopping myself mid-sentence from letting loose something nasty (which happened from time to time, even in church).

As strange and humorous that some of that sounds, I was desperate for stability. God and His word became an anchor to my wounded soul. Like Odysseus who had his men tie him to the mast so he would not listen to the Sirens luring his ship to smash into the rocky shore. I also lashed myself to God and His word so I would not self-destruct.

Radical Transformation

Well-meaning people would try to talk me down from my radical transformation; they would say misguided things like:

"You don't have to be so extreme."

"You can still be a Christian and not be so fanatical."

"If you read your Bible too much, you'll go insane."

They didn't understand that I had a true "born again" experience and was on fire for God. I want you to know that people CAN change and be given a new lease on life. It happened to me, and if it happened to me it can happen to anyone. If you are desperate to see supernatural, positive changes in your life, turn to Jesus whole heartedly and He will hear your deepest cry and longing. It's time for you to have a radical transformation.

If you are desperate for a transformation, and you believe with all your heart that Jesus died for your sins and rose from the dead so that you can have newness of life, then pray this prayer:

Dear Lord Jesus,
I know that I am a sinner, and I ask you for your forgiveness. I believe You died for my sins and rose from the dead. I turn from my sins and invite You to come into my heart and life. I want to trust and follow You as Lord and Savior.
In Your Name, Amen

For whoever calls on the name of the Lord shall be saved.
~Romans 10:13

SPIRIT WORLD

If you said that prayer and meant it, then you are now born again. The Holy Spirit dwells in your heart and will bear witness with your spirit that you are a child of God.

> *For you did not receive the spirit of bondage again to fear, but you received the Spirit of adoption by whom we cry out, "Abba, Father." The Spirit Himself bears witness with our spirit that we are children of God.* ~Romans 8:15-16

Now that you have made a decision to follow Christ, it's important for you to grow spiritually. To do that you must read your Bible daily and find a solid church in your area that teaches the full Gospel of Christ. You must surround yourself with Christians of like faith who will encourage you. Someone who is recovering from an addiction must attend a support group regularly. The church is your support group and you must develop a lifestyle of faithful attendance and service. God is working in you and has a great purpose for you.

Read your Bible:

> *As newborn babes, desire the pure milk of the word, that you may grow thereby.* ~ Peter 2:2

Go to church regularly:

> *And let us consider one another in order to stir up love and good works, not forsaking the assembling of ourselves together, as is the manner of some, but exhorting one another, and so much the more as you see the Day approaching.* ~Hebrews 10:24-25

You are saved to serve: God has good works for you to do. He has a plan and a purpose for your life that will unfold as you follow Him.

Radical Transformation

For by grace you have been saved through faith, and that not of yourselves; it is the gift of God, not of works, lest anyone should boast. **For we are His workmanship, created in Christ Jesus for good works, which God prepared beforehand that we should walk in them.** ~Ephesians 2:8-10

For I know the plans I have for you, declares the Lord, plans to prosper you and not to harm you, plans to give you hope and a future. *Then you will call on me and come and pray to me, and I will listen to you. You will seek me and find me when you seek me with all your heart.* ~Jeremiah 29:11-13 NIV

www.ingramcontent.com/pod-product-compliance
Lightning Source LLC
Chambersburg PA
CBHW071353290426
44108CB00014B/1525